G000243871

Roses for an Empress

Rosa Damascena

l'impératrice Joséphine
dessinée d'après
nature
par David

Donné à mon fils
Eugène
Davioß

Roses for an Empress

Josephine Bonaparte
& Pierre-Joseph Redouté

SIDGWICK & JACKSON
LONDON

Page 2, The Empress Josephine, drawing by Jacques-Louis David, with the inscription donné à mon fils Eugène *(for my son Eugène), Musée National de Malmaison*

The letters of Napoleon on pages 46 and 86 and the first letter on page 60 are taken from *Napoleon's Letters*, edited by J. M. Thompson (Dent, London 1954).

The quotations from the *Memoirs of Madame de La Tour de Pin* on pages 15 and 69 are taken from Felice Harcourt's edition (Harvill Press, London 1969).

The letter from Alexandre de Beauharnais's superiors on page 33 and the petition on page 36 are taken from Hubert Cole, *Josephine* (Heinemann, London 1962).

The quotation from the ode by Anacreon on page 118 is taken from the translation of *The Anacreontea* by Judson France Davidson (Dent, London 1915).

The verses on pages 6, 18, 30, 42, 58, 82, 102 are taken from *Les Jardins ou l'art d'embellir les paysages* by Jacques Delille (Paris 1782), translated by Maria H. Montolieu (T. Bensley, London 1798).

Translated by Anna Bennett

First published in Great Britain in 1983 by Sidgwick and Jackson Limited

Copyright © 1982 Arnoldo Mondadori Editore S.p.A., Milan
English translation copyright © 1983 Arnoldo Mondadori Editore S.p.A., Milan
Illustrations copyright © 1980 Harenberg Kommunikation, Dortmund

First published in Italy in 1982 under the title *Le Rose dell'Imperatrice* by Arnoldo Mondadori Editore S.p.A., Milan

ISBN 0–283–98983–1

Printed and bound in Italy by Officine Grafiche di Arnoldo Mondadori Editore, Verona
for Sidgwick and Jackson Limited
1 Tavistock Chambers, Bloomsbury Way
London WC1A 2SG

Rosa Damascena Italica

Josephine Bonaparte had more than two hundred varieties of roses in the magnificent gardens of her palace at Malmaison: Rosa gallica, Rosa centifolia, Rosa alba, *China roses, damask roses. . . . A few years before her death she asked Pierre-Joseph Redouté, known as the 'Raphael of flowers', to capture their ephemeral beauty with his paintbrush.*

These are Josephine's roses, painted by Redouté – the roses the Empress was never to see. And this is the story, through the eyes of her contemporaries in memoirs, letters, and documents, of the incomparable Josephine herself, to whom General Bonaparte had written from the battlefields of Italy:

"My heart has no feelings anywhere other than where you reign, no thoughts that are not subordinated to you. My strength, my arms, my spirit are yours. My soul rests within your body. The day when you will change or cease to live shall be the day of my death. Nature and the world I behold are beautiful only because you dwell therein. . . ."

A h! lorsque d'un long deuil la terre enfin respire,
Dans les champs, dans les bois, sur les monts d'alentour,
Quand tout rit de bonheur, d'esperance et d'amour,
Qu'un autre ouvre aux grands noms les fastes de la gloire;
Sur un char foudroyant qu'il place la victoire;
Que la coupe d'Atrée ensanglante ses mains:
Flore a souri; ma voix va chanter les jardins.

Ah! when Earth throws her mourning garb away,
When hills, and meads, and every verdant grove,
Smile with reviving hope, and joy, and love,
Let others celebrate the pomp of war,
Place glorious Victory on her thundering car,
Let Atreus' cup their hands with crimson stain,
Flora invites, I sing her lovely reign.

From Delille, *Les Jardins*, I

The Young Girl from Martinique

1763–1779

Rosa Centifolia

Rosa Moschata

Rosa Gallica latifolia

arie-Joseph-Rose Tascher de La Pagerie was born on 23 June 1763 at the de Sanois plantation, which belonged to her mother, in the village of Trois-Ilets, Martinique, in the West Indies. The mulatto and negro slave women on the plantation called her Yeyette, a corruption of Rosette. When she was a young girl of fourteen, in 1777, Count Montgaillard, an officer in the Auxerrois regiment on garrison duty on the island, made her acquaintance and described the effect she had on him.

"She possessed in great measure the power to charm and the visual advantages that draw compliments, seduce the soul and make hearts flutter; nature had blessed her with many attractions. Without being beautiful, without even being what one might describe as pretty,

Mlle de la Pagerie was remarkable for a certain fascination and a disarming expression. Her appearance embraced both voluptuousness and an indefinable caressing look that appealed to the soul and, above all, addressed itself to the senses. Her figure was that of a nymph; her entire person bore the mark of the vivacity, the freedom, the abandon that only Creole women know how to combine in their movements, their manners, their tone of voice, even their silences. Josephine was by nature good, stubborn, inconsiderate, astonishingly coquettish, and of a flightiness of taste and feeling that would tolerate no contradictions."

Rosa Rubrifolia

Rosa centifolia Bullata

osephine's daughter Hortense recalled her mother telling of a prediction made by an old negress in Martinique before her wedding. After foretelling an extraordinary future for her, including two marriages far away from the colony, and two children by her first husband, the woman had added that Josephine would have become more than a queen but she must beware a priest who would seek her downfall. It is not difficult to interpret the prophecy: Alexandre de Beauharnais and Napoleon Bonaparte are the two husbands; Eugène and Hortense her children; and the priest-turned-statesman Talleyrand, possibly, the priest.

The soothsayer was called Eliama and she also read the hand of another young girl, a distant relation of Josephine's named Aimée du Duc de Rivery, telling her that she would one day be a 'veiled queen'. Baron Ménéval, secretary to Napoleon Bonaparte, wrote of how the girl was captured at sea by pirates and believed to have been taken to the harem at Constantinople where she supposedly became the Sultan's favourite and mother to his heir. When her alleged grandson, the Turkish Sultan Abdul Aziz, visited the 1867 Exposition Universelle in Paris he met Napoleon III and reminded the Emperor, himself the grandson of Josephine, of this unusual – but only legendary – family relationship.

At the time of Marie-Joseph-Rose Tascher de la Pagerie's birth Louis XV reigned in France, as – in a different sense – did Madame de Pompadour. Carlo Maria Buonaparte, a Corsican by birth and descended from the Italian nobility, was seventeen and about to become a lawyer. The following year he was to marry Letizia Ramolino, the daughter of a general inspector of roads and bridges in Corsica, who would bear him thirteen children, one of whom was christened Napoleone.

The set of circumstances that would link the destinies of these two families had already been established. On 13 May 1757 François de Beauharnais, a forty-three-year-old naval commander, had arrived in Martinique as Governor and Lieutenant-General of the islands (then all known by their French names) of Martinique, Guadeloupe, Marie-Galande, St-Martin, St-Barthélemy, La Desiderade, La Dominique, Ste-Lucie, La Grenade, Les Grenadins, Tobago, St-Vincent, Cayenne with its dependencies and the Windward Islands of America. This officer from Orleans, who had never fired a single cannon-ball, was expected to defend the French colonies in the Caribbean against attacks by the British (the Seven Years War was just beginning). Beauharnais soon welcomed into his circle Gaspard-Joseph Tascher de la Pagerie, who was also from Orleans. Gaspard came from the impoverished nobility; his family had been in Martinique since 1726, having gone there in the vain hope of making their fortune. His son Joseph-Gaspard was a lieutenant in the coastal artillery; one of his daughters, Marie-Euphémie-Désirée, aged eighteen, became the Governor's wife's companion, then mistress of the Governor himself. Gaspard-Joseph, Joseph-Gaspard and Marie-Euphémie-Désirée would become Josephine's grandfather, father and aunt respectively.

In March 1759 a British naval force attacked Guadeloupe. The Governor arrived on the scene too late, only to find that the island had already surrendered. Malicious gossip attributed his delay to his insistence on attending the wedding of his mistress and his aide-de-camp Alexis-Michel-Auguste Renaudin, who had been imprisoned for four years in the fortress of Saumur in France, accused through a *lettre de cachet*, written secretly by an enemy, of having poisoned his father. The following year Mme Renaudin was godmother to the son, Alexandre-François-Marie, that the Governor had meanwhile had by his wife, and she left the same day for France, where her husband had preceded her. During separation proceedings which were to be dragged out for twelve years he accused his wife of notoriously bad behaviour, and she accused him in turn of attempting to poison her.

Having been replaced as Governor, Beauharnais followed his mistress a year later, in April 1761, lived with her and finally married her when she was widowed thirty-five years later, in 1796. His governorship had not been an illustrious one, but he was nonetheless awarded a pension by the King, and the title of Marquis de la Ferté-Beauharnais. His son Alexandre, considered too young to face the discomfort of an

Rosa Berberifolia

Rosa Lucida

Rosa Bracteata

Rosa Eglanteria
var. punicea

Atlantic crossing, stayed behind for a few years in Martinique and was looked after by Mme Renaudin's mother, who was to become Josephine's grandmother.

Shortly after Beauharnais' departure the dashing young gunnery officer Joseph-Gaspard de la Pagerie married Rose-Claire des Vergers de Sanois on 9 November 1761. She brought with her 18,000 livres in cash, a promised income and the plantation at Trois-Ilets. The marriage produced three daughters: Marie-Joseph-Rose, born in 1763; Catherine-Désirée, born on 11 December 1764; and Marie-Françoise, born on 3 September 1766.

Rosa Pomponia

Rosa Montezuma

he Marquis de la Ferté-Beauharnais, former Governor of Martinique, wrote from France in October 1777 to Joseph-Gaspard Tascher de la Pagerie at the Trois-Ilets:

"At present my children enjoy an income of 40,000 livres each. You are free to send me Mlle your daughter so that she may share my son's fortune; the respect and affection he feels for Mme Renaudin makes him ardently wish to marry one of her nieces. I am doing no more, believe me, than acceding to her request that I should ask you for your second daughter, since her age is quite close to his. . . . I should have been much happier were your eldest daughter some years younger: she would certainly have been preferred, since I have been given an equally favourable account of her. But I must confess that my son, who is only seventeen and a half, thinks that a young woman of fifteen is too close in age to him. This is one of those occasions when wise parents are forced to bow to circumstances."

Mme Renaudin described to her brother the future bridegroom, her godson Alexandre-François-Marie de Beauharnais, who, although born in Martinique, had moved to France at the age of ten:

"A pleasing countenance, a charming appearance, spirit, wit and, the most priceless gift of all, he encompasses all the best qualities of heart and mind within his person; he is well loved by all who surround him."

Sadly, the second of the Tascher de la Pagerie daughters died of a fever a few days before the Marquis sent his marriage proposal. This left the third daughter, of whom Tascher wrote of the Marquis in 1778:

"She is eleven and a half years old. Her goodness and cheerfulness of character are reflected in a face which will develop attractively, and I hope that with the addition of a good education she will be worthy of your affection and of your son."

The third daughter, Marie-Françoise, at first agreed to the match, though only reluctantly, then would hear nothing of it. Another objection was the fact that her mother did not want to be parted from her. The eldest daughter Marie-Joseph-Rose, on the other hand, cherished dreams of France and Paris. In June 1778 her father wrote to the Marquis about this problem:

"The eldest girl, who left the convent some time ago and has for a long time frequently asked me to take her to France, will, I fear, be somewhat affected by the preference which I appear to give to her younger sister. She has a very fine skin, beautiful eyes, beautiful arms and a surprising inclination towards music. I allowed her a guitar teacher during the time she was at the convent; she has benefited from it and has a pretty voice. It is a pity that she has not had the benefit of an education in France, and if it were left to me I would bring you two daughters instead of one. But how can one part a mother from the two daughters who remain to her at the moment when death has just deprived her of the third?"

'Come with one of your daughters or with both,' wrote Mme Renaudin to her brother, and continued:

"Anything that you do will be agreeable to us, and please believe that we leave you to be guided by Providence, which knows better than we do what is good for us. You know our real feelings; the sad event which has just occurred only increases our eagerness. We must have one of your children."

Meanwhile, the future bridegroom had written to his father:

"It cannot surely be your intention to make me marry this young lady, should she and I take a mutual dislike to each other?"

They received the Marquis's permission to publish the banns, with a blank space for the name of the bride.

Almost another year had elapsed, however, on account of military commitments which Tascher de la Pagerie had to keep in the defence of the islands, and lack of funds, before he, his daughter Marie-Joseph-Rose and the mulatto maid Euphémie finally boarded the *Ile-de-France*.

Rosa Indica acuminata

Rosa Indica

"**M**lle Tascher will perhaps appear to you less pretty than you had expected, but I think I may assure you that the frankness and sweetness of her nature will surpass what you have been told."

Thus Alexandre wrote to his father soon after meeting his sixteen-year-old fiancée, who had disembarked at Brest on 12 October 1779, indisposed by the rigours of the journey.

Alexandre was nineteen and a captain in the Sarre infantry regiment, commanded by the Duc de la Rochefoucauld, a mason and a great liberal thinker and philanthropist. Alexandre had taken the title Vicomte de Beauharnais, even though he was only entitled to the lower rank of Chevalier. In any case the nobility of the Beauharnais was doubtful, apart from the title of Marquis which

Rosa Muscosa multiplex

Rosa Alpina Laevis

had been recently conferred on the former Governor of Martinique and which was to be inherited by the first-born son, François. When the Duc de Coligny sought an admission to court for Alexandre, he received the following reply from the genealogist of the various noble Orders:

"M. de Beauharnais is not worthy of the court honours he seeks. The family is a good bourgeois one from Orleans, which, so an ancient family tree in the Cabinet of the Order of the Holy Ghost tells us, was formerly known under the name Beauvit. Some of its members have been merchants, Knights, Commanders and deputies at the presidential seat of the city itself, others were councillors at the Parliament in Paris. One of the family's branches, known by the name of La Bretsche, was charged on 4 April 1667, under judgement of M. Machault, the inspector of

Orleans, with usurping its nobility, and fined 2000 livres, a penalty which was then reduced to 1000 livres."

The marriage contract was drawn up in Paris on 10 December and the wedding took place on 13 December 1779 at Noisy-le-Grand. The young couple set up home in the Rue Thévenot in Paris, in the house of the Marquis de la Ferté-Beauharnais.

 eyette the Creole, now Vicomtesse de Beauharnais, was at last in Paris. It was only her husband, however, who led a dazzling social life. As the Marquise de la Tour du Pin would later write:

"Between 1787 and 1791 I used to see M. de Beauharnais daily in fashionable society. As he had also seen a great deal of M. de la Tour du Pin while my husband was aide-de-camp to M. de Bouillé during the American War [of Independence], M. de Beauharnais asked him to call so that he might meet his wife. M. de la Tour du Pin did call on them once, but not again. They moved in different circles from ours. M. de Beauharnais, however, was accepted everywhere, for during the war he had become acquainted with many of the highest in the land. He was a handsomely built man and in those days, when dancing was considered an art, he was thought – and with some reason – to be the finest dancer in Paris. I had often danced with him myself, so that when I heard of his death on the scaffold I was much affected. I could not imagine him elsewhere than in a quadrille . . . a bitter contrast!"

Rosa Indica vulgaris

Rosa Centifolia mutabilis

artinique, in the lesser Antilles, is at the centre of the cluster of small islands, known as the West Indies, which stretches from Puerto Rico to the South American coast and seals off the Caribbean on the east. A mountainous, volcanic island, thick with humid equatorial forest it is some 2,600 square miles in size – roughly five times the size of the island of Elba.

Christopher Columbus discovered it, arriving there on 13 June 1502 during his fourth and final voyage. The Spaniards did not stay long because of the hostility of the Carib natives. The French arrived in 1635 and remained there, even when the island was attacked by the Dutch in 1674 and occupied by the British in 1762, 1794 and 1809.

To the newcomer Martinique gives the impression of being an earthly paradise. A nineteenth-century civil servant described his arrival on the island thus:

"It is dazzling. The sea is purest silver; it shimmers with the smoothness of a mirror, speckled here and there with little boats drawing near under the sun, rowed by naked natives: ... a multitude of luxuriant little islands, like tufts of greenery, sprouts from the water around us. A prodigious vegetation envelops the city which stretches to the shore. This is the happiest picture of the Antilles, a triumph of greenery, golden sunlight and shimmering sea...."

Slaves were imported to work on the plantations, most particularly on the sugar plantations. Since the second half of the seventeenth century sugar cane had become the major crop, surpassing even tobacco in importance. At the time of Josephine's birth, the island contained no fewer than 65,000 slaves out of a total population of about 80,000. The other inhabitants were mostly French; being born in the colonies they were known as Creoles, a term of Spanish origin meaning a home-produced chicken.

Opposite above: The house where
Josephine lived in Martinique. It was
called successively Le Moulin à sucre, La
Sucrerie de la petite Guinée, Le Sanois, and
finally La Pagerie from the family's name.
Opposite below: Fort-Royal, now Fort-de-
France, on the island of Martinique.

*Milastre qui fume, et qui est vestu de la maniere que les
mulastres esclaves sont venus dans les Isles françoises de
l'amerique.*

Right: A mulatto slave from the French
Antilles.
Below: The bay of Fort-Royal in 1666,
'en l'estat quil étoit lors de la guerre
avec l'Angleterre' (as it was during the
war with England). The three little
islands in the bottom right-hand corner, the
Trois-Ilets, give their name to the area on
the coast overlooking them, where the
Tascher plantation was situated.

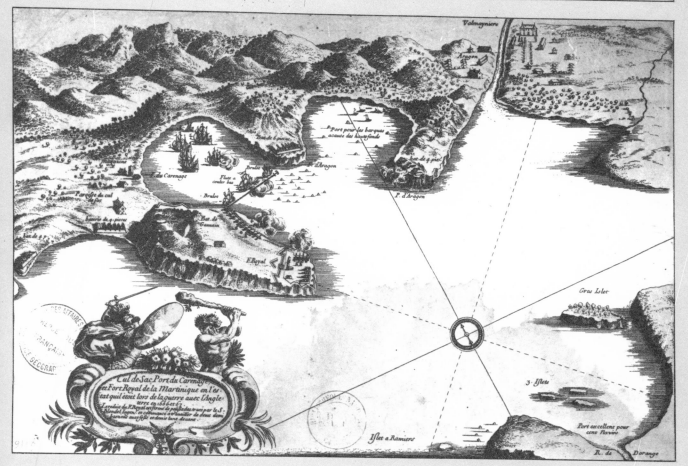

Mais qui peut refuser un hommage à la rose,
La rose, dont Vénus compose ses bosquets,
Le printemps sa guirlande, et l'Amour ses bouquets . . .
Fleurs charmantes! par vous la nature est plus belle;
Dans ses brillans tableaux l'art vous prend pour modèle;
Simples tributs du coeur, vos dons sont chaque jour
Offerts par l'amitié, hasardés par l'amour.
D'embellir la beauté vous obtenez la gloire;
Le laurier vous permet de parer la victoire . . .
L'autel même où de Dieu repose la grandeur,
Se parfume au printemps de vos douces offrandes . . .
Mais c'est dans nos jardins qu'est votre heureux séjour.
Filles de la rosée et de l'astre du jour . . .

Yet who denies a tribute to the rose?
The rose Anacreon sung, and at the feast
A crown of roses Horace's temples graced,
Love forms his posies, Venus decks her bowers,
Spring weaves fresh garlands with these favoured flowers . . .
Nature more beauteous seems adorned with flowers;
To paint their colours Art exerts her powers;
Affection's simple token still they prove,
Offered by Friendship, hazarded by Love;
The laurel lets them in their glory share;
Their pride it is to ornament the fair . . .
Sweet, from the altar where to God we bend,
In Spring their perfumes unto Heaven ascend . . .
But in our gardens is their true abode.
Daughter of Phoebus and the dewy Morn . . .

From Delille, *Les Jardins*, III

The Vicomtesse de Beauharnais

1779–1790

Rosa Sulfurea

About her education, Alexandre de Beauharnais wrote to his wife:

"I am very taken with your desire for education. This proclivity, which we can always indulge, is a source of chaste enjoyment and has the prized advantage of leaving no regret if pursued. It is by persisting in your resolve that the knowledge you will acquire will elevate you above others and, by marrying science and modesty, will make you a truly accomplished woman. The talents you cultivate also have their own charm, and by sacrificing a part of your day you will be able to combine the useful with the pleasant."

Rosa Villosa, Pomifera

Rosa Kamtschatica

To Patricol, his former tutor, Alexandre wrote:

"At the sight of Mlle de la Pagerie I felt I could live happily with her; I at once devised a plan to reform her education and zealously to make good the omissions of those first fifteen years of her life that had been so neglected. Soon after our marriage, however, I discovered in her a lack of trust which astonished me, although I did everything to inspire this sentiment in her. . . . I confess that this discovery has somewhat dampened my enthusiasm as regards her instruction. . . . Instead of spending a large part of my time at home, with someone who has nothing to say to me, I frequently go out, more than I had planned to do, and have taken up some of my former life as a bachelor. I do not renounce easily that happiness which the idea of a good marriage seemed to promise me. Although I have given myself up greatly to mundane matters, I have not lost my taste for work. I am ready to choose domestic happiness and peace before the riotous pleasures of society. However, behaving as I did, I fancied that my wife – had she felt genuine friendship towards me – would strive to draw me closer to her, and to acquire those qualities which I admire and which would hold me in check. Not so! The very opposite has happened; instead of seeing my wife turn to learning and skills, she has become jealous, assuming all the characteristics peculiar to this confounded emotion.

That is the state of affairs we find ourselves in at the present moment; she wants me to devote myself to her exclusively; she wants to know what I say, what I do, what I write, and she does not think of winning that trust which I regret I cannot give her, but would gladly grant her if she would only show willing in making herself more cultured and more appealing."

The couple had two children, Eugène, born 3 September 1781, and Hortense, born 10 April 1783, but parted even before their daughter's birth. On 26 September 1782 Alexandre sailed from Brest on board the *Vénus*, bound for Martinique and military glory in America, where France and Britain were fighting over colonies. His former mistress Laure de Girardin, the widowed Mme Longpré, was a passenger on the same boat.

Rosa Clynophylla

Rosa Gallica officinalis

Rosa Damascena subalba

Rosa Muscosa anemoneflora

Once he had arrived in Martinique Alexandre wrote in these terms to his wife on 8 July 1783:

"Had I written to you in the first rush of my anger, my pen would have burned through the paper and you would certainly have believed, in bearing the full brunt of my invective, that I had chosen a moment of temper or jealousy with which to write to you; however, I have known what I have to say to you, or at least part of it, for more than three weeks now. Thus, in spite of the desperation that assails my soul, despite the rage which threatens to choke me, I will contain myself, and tell you in cold blood that you are in my sight the vilest of all creatures, and that my sojourn in this country has taught me the abominable behaviour you indulged in here; I now know every single detail of your intrigue with M. de B., an officer in the Martinique regiment, and of your liaison with M. d'H., who serves on board the *César*. I am conversant with the means whereby you procured your satisfaction, as well as the people you found to provide you with the opportunity for such satisfaction. . . . There is therefore no reason to pursue this pretence any further, and since I am familiar with all the facts, there is only one course of action left open to you, that of good faith.

As to repentance, I ask for none; you are incapable of it. A creature who while making arrangements for the journey to her fiancé could welcome a lover into her arms has no conscience: she is lower than the lowest fiends on earth. . . . After so much misdemeanour and cruelty, what am I to think of the dark clouds, the disputes that have overshadowed our marriage? What am I to

Rosa Eglanteria

Rosa Indica fragrans

think of this latest infant [Hortense], who arrived only eight months and a few days after my return from Italy? I am obliged to recognize the child, but I swear by God above that it is not mine; a stranger's blood flows through its veins! This child will never be aware of my shame and, I swear, will never know, through her education and financial security, that she is the fruit of an adulterous liaison, but you will appreciate my pains to avoid such a shocking event happening again in the future.

The choice is yours: I will never again place myself in a position where I may be duped, and since you are not above deceiving me under my own roof, please be good enough to take yourself to a convent as soon as this letter reaches you; this is my last word on the matter, and nothing on earth will make me revoke this decision."

At Fort-Royal Laure Girardin, who had friends and relatives in Martinique, had collected some choice morsels of gossip. Alexandre had at once hurried to the Trois-Ilets to bribe the slaves and servants on the Sanois plantation. Some rejected him with scorn, but others supplied further confirmatory tales. Alexandre also had an altercation with his father-in-law, who was to write to him in these terms:

"So this is the fruit of your journey and the fine campaign you planned against the enemies of the state. You are reduced to waging war against your wife's reputation and her family's peace of mind."

Rosa Centifolia carnea

Rosa Centifolia simplex

would never have dreamt that the viscount, our son-in-law, would have heaped such afflictions upon us. . . . He twice gave the slave fifteen *moëde*. What slave would not yield to temptation when offered such a sum of money, and what slave would not indeed sell his masters for half that amount? He is held in chains at the moment. I would dearly love to send him to you so you might interrogate him. . . . How could such a disgrace, brought about by such vile means, have been perpetrated by so cultured and well-born a gentleman? It is hardly likely that my daughter would wish to stay with him, that she could continue to live with a husband who is so weak as to cover himself with shame in order to purchase his wife's dishonour.''

Thus wrote Marie-Joseph-Rose's mother to the Marquis de Beauharnais.

On his return from Martinique Alexandre landed at Rochefort on 15 September 1783. Attempts at a reconciliation were to prove abortive, even though his father took his wife's part. Alexandre refused Marie-Joseph-Rose access to the house, selling all its contents, so that she finally was forced to retire to a convent in Paris as legal proceedings got under way. She was able to allege that out of two years and nine months of marriage, her husband had only spent ten months with her. The case was closed on 4 March 1785: having been unable to produce any evidence, Alexandre withdrew his accusations and agreed to a separation on his wife's terms.

he convent where the Vicomtesse de Beauharnais spent fifteen months was run by the energetic Abbess Marie-Catherine de Béthisy de Mézières, and was actually a pleasant and orderly residence for widowed gentlewomen, ladies awaiting legal separation from their husbands, elderly spinsters or orphaned girls awaiting husbands. Here Marie-Joseph-Rose completed the mundane side of her education, enjoying those social relationships she had not been able to take advantage of during her colonial adolescence and, subsequently, during her lonely marriage to the 'finest dancer in Paris'.

Rosa Pimpinellifolia Mariaeburgensis

Rosa Carolina Corymbosa

When she left the convent Marie-Joseph-Rose went to live in Fontainebleau with her father-in-law and aunt. Even during this period she is said to have had lovers, but in June 1788 she left for Martinique with her daughter Hortense.

ocumentary evidence of this period in her life exists in the form of the following recollections written by the second officer of the brig *Levrette*, which put into port at Fort-Royal in August 1789:

"My first concern, having landed, was to call on some old acquaintances, whose polite welcome was always such a pleasure. I must mention M. and Mme Tascher de la Pagerie [namely Baron Tascher, the port commander and Marie-Joseph-Rose's uncle, and his wife], at whose house I happened to meet Mme de Beauharnais, who would later play such an important role in our illegitimate pomp. This lady, without being exactly attractive, was pleasing by virtue of her manner, her gaiety and her kind-heartedness. More concerned with seeking those pleasures to which she was to some extent entitled through her age and charms, she quite publicly challenged any more or less favourable opinion one may have entertained of her. However, because her funds were extremely limited and she loved spending money, she was frequently obliged to resort to the purse of her admirers."

25

In 1790 the French Revolution spread to Martinique. As Hortense recorded in her memoirs:

"The Revolution was making itself felt in the colony. M. de Viomesnil and then M. de Damas had been governors, but Damas was forced to leave in a hurry. We were staying at the Petit Gouvernement. One evening my mother was informed that the following morning gunfire would spread throughout Fort-Royal. She instantly sought refuge in a frigate whose captain she was acquainted with [Durant d'Ubraye, who commanded the naval division of the Windward Islands on garrison duty in Martinique]. As we were crossing the Savane meadow a cannon-ball fell quite close to us.

The following day the rebels, who had by now conquered the city, ordered the French vessels to turn back, threatening them with all the artillery the fort possessed. The crew shouted that they wanted to return to France. We promptly set sail, leaving the coast behind, but the threat was nevertheless carried out and cannon shots were fired; fortunately, fate spared us and none of them hit us. So there we were, suddenly on board ship, having bid no one farewell, and on our way to France without ever having intended to do so.

The frigate we were sailing in was called the *Sensible* and she was bound for Toulon. The crossing seemed to be going well when the navigating officer made an error and directed us towards Africa. We touched the coastline and five minutes later the frigate ran aground. Everyone – sailors, passengers, children – pulled on the ropes, and once again we were spared from danger.

On her arrival in Toulon [29 October 1790] my mother learned of the events which were shaking France. The Revolution had broken out and my father was already playing a prominent role in the party he had joined. His brother had chosen a different one. My grandfather had retired to Fontainebleau with his old friend Mme de Renaudin, my mother's aunt. We went there at once and shortly afterwards my brother [Eugène], who was at college in Harcourt, joined us.

At Fontainebleau was born the harmony of feelings that made us permanent friends ... in fortune as in misfortune, making us interpret life's events from the same viewpoint. We could not foresee the dazzling and turbulent future that lay ahead of us, but seeing each other again after an interval of a few years, even though both of us were still children [Eugène was nine, Hortense seven], we found that events had already overtaken us. We related these events to each other in detail; I told him of our journey to America, the negroes' rebellion, our hasty escape, the dangers we had faced when the frigate we were travelling in came under attack by cannon fire, and the risk of shipwreck we had undergone on the African coast. He had not had as much experience of life as me at this time; he had no inkling then that fate would one day send him to the desert sands, as it would to the ice and snow of Russia. A simple schoolboy, settled at college in Harcourt, he agreed that my adventures were more tragic than his had been."

Rosa Rubiginosa triflora

Rosa Redutea rubescens

Rosa Muscosa alba

Rosa Pimpinellifolia Pumila

Many years later Durant d'Ubraye, requesting a pension from the Navy minister, was to recall these events.

"The kindness with which Her Majesty the Empress and Princess Louis [Hortense, now wife of Louis Bonaparte] wish to honour me gives me the boldness to lay before you the only truly happy event to come my way in fifteen years. In 1790, as commander of the naval forces on garrison duty on the Windward Islands, during a moment of terrifying insurrection, I was happy to welcome on board the frigate *Sensible* Her Majesty the Empress and Princess Louis, her daughter, and to take them back to France."

The Emperor agreed to the pension, though it was not a generous one.

Left, young girls in flowing, diaphanous Empire style dresses, turbans, and headdresses decorated with feathers and stars, playing blind-man's-buff. Opposite, the magic lantern, carefully operated by a surly old woman. The purpose behind this print is a didactic one; the scenes projected on to the sheet are: 'The unpretentious artist, the hard-working young girl, the young scholar, a mother teaching her child.'

At the end of the Revolutionary Wars there was still time for leisure among those social classes who had really nothing whatever to do. 'Society' filled the days of whoever was involved in it. Josephine's first husband basked in it; she herself would have been greedy for such pleasures, but Alexandre preferred her to devote her time to filling in the gaps left by her 'colonial' education with texts that his own tutor, Patricol, had used to shape his mind. Alexandre's learning, moulded by

Left, a game of badminton. Opposite, a game of hide-and-seek. All these illustrations are taken from Bon Genre, a collection of satirical coloured prints, published in Paris between 1801 and 1817.

such texts, was characterized by a plethora of nouns requiring capital letters, and by a latent tendency towards pompous pronouncements.

Josephine's second husband would have no such prejudices against his wife. He preferred to play instead.

The games he favoured were highly active ones, turning grown-up people into a troupe of schoolchildren on the lawns of Malmaison, always with an edge of violence. Bonaparte loved to bend rules to his own advantage and it may well be that these games con-

tributed in their own way to his legend.

They also played very old games which have lasted until today, such as blind-man's-buff, badminton, and hide-and-seek. They would possibly also have marvelled at the forerunner of the photographic or electronic picture, the old magic lantern, with a touch of didactic pedantry.

Laure Junot, later the Duchesse d'Abrantès, one day spotted a stranger spying on the gardens at Malmaison. Josephine took fright, but Bonaparte recognized the man as a veteran who had lost an arm at the Battle of Marengo. 'It was quite extraordinary', the old man remarked, observing the rustic entertainment at Malmaison, 'to see the First Consul amuse himself like the poorest Frenchman in the Republic.'

Cards too were a universal pastime. Napoleon never played for money, but invariably cheated. Josephine would engage in endless solitaires, believing the outcome of them to have some divinatory significance. Plays were also put on at Malmaison, performed for Napoleon by Laure Junot and her husband, Eugène de Beauharnais, Bourrienne (Bonaparte's secretary) and even Cambacérès, the Second Consul, cast in the role of the nobleman father.

Josephine loved flowers and during her latter years became a botany enthusiast. She grew unknown exotic plants in the greenhouses at Malmaison, which court botanists classified with her name (*La Pageria, Bonapartea* or *Josephina imperatrix*), and also introduced to France eucalyptus, hibiscus, camellias, different varieties of myrtle, geraniums, mimosa, cacti, rhododendrons, dahlias, rare tulips and hyacinths; the hydrangea, *hortense* in French, derived its name from her daughter. However, as Méneval, another of Napoleon's secretaries, wrote, above all 'she loved luxury, and spending money'.

antôt, dans le lointain confuse et fugitive,
Se déploie une riche et vaste perspective.
Quelquefois un bosquet riant, mais recueilli,
Par la nature et vous à la fois embelli,
Plein d'ombres et de fleurs, et d'un luxe champêtre,
Semble dire : 'Arrêtez ; ou pouvez-vous mieux être ?'

Soft where the distances recede, behold
Half veiled in mist perspectives wide unfold,
While near a bower attractive, and retired,
in Art's and Nature's choicest gifts attired,
Adorned with shrubs and flowers, appears to say,
'What seek ye more? Here, here contented stay!'

From Delille, *Les Jardins*, IV

Revolution and Terror:
Citizeness Beauharnais

1790–1794

Rosa Gallica Versicolor

Rosa Brevistyla Leucochroa

Rosa Damaxena Coccinea

Rosa Alba regalis

Both the Beauharnais brothers had been elected to represent the nobility at the Estates-General of 1789, Alexandre in Blois and François in Paris. Eugène de Beauharnais recalls in his memoirs:

"I remember attending many sittings of the Constituent Assembly, where my father, who had embraced the principles of the Revolution, sat on the left side, while his elder brother, the Marquis François de Beauharnais, sat on the right. Sometimes I would sit by the stove which was at the centre of the hall where the meetings were held, one hand in my father's hand and the other in my uncle's, without them exchanging a single word."

Alexandre had been one of the forty-seven members of the nobility who, by means of the Oath of the Tennis Court, had voted on 20 June 1789 for union with the third estate, and on 4 August he was among those who voted for the renunciation of feudal rights. As the Vicomte de

Vogüé wrote:

"Seeing him go about his business of national destruction, one would say that Josephine's first husband works harder than any of his accomplices to pave the way for the exploits and good fortune of her second husband."

ortense recalled:

"Since I was too young at the time to understand what was happening around me, my memory has only retained a few events. At the time of the King's departure and his arrest at Varennes [June 1791], my father was president of the Constituent Assembly. His steadfastness and the influence this brought to bear on the tranquillity of the capital whipped up a feeling of enthusiasm throughout Paris. Even in our retreat at Fontainebleau, when people saw my brother and me they would exclaim: 'There go our new Dauphin and Dauphine.'"

Rosa Redutea glauca

ince the Constituent Assembly forbade the re-election of its members Alexandre returned to the army, moving from active service to the administration of the war archives. He became General Adjutant Lieutenant-Colonel on 23 May 1792; Field-Marshal on 7 September that year; Lieutenant-General on 8 March 1793; and was provisionally designated General-in-Chief on the following 23 May 1793. Offered the post of Minister of War on 13 June, he refused, saying: 'With my principles, commanding is nothing, whereas the honour of defending my country is everything.' As far as military operations were concerned, his task was to release Mainz, which was then under siege. On 28 July 1793 the National Convention learned that Mainz had surrendered on the 23rd. Beauharnais resigned, which provoked the following letter from his superiors.

"The representatives of the people with the Army of the Rhine: Considering that the General-in-Chief Beauharnais has constantly repeated his offer to resign, both by word of mouth and in writing; considering that, in the opinion of many, he has neither the strength nor the moral energy necessary to a Republican General-in-Chief; considering that his state of weakness and languor, which have kept him away from the army during three days of battle, can only produce distrust and discouragement in the general staff of the army: we order that his resignation shall be accepted and that he shall within the space of six hours remove himself a distance of one hundred miles from the frontiers to a place of residence which he shall notify to us and to the National Convention."

One of the three signatories added: 'I would have been in favour of arresting Beauharnais.'

Rosa foetida

Rosa Cinnamomea | flore simplici

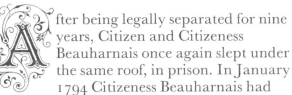

After being legally separated for nine years, Citizen and Citizeness Beauharnais once again slept under the same roof, in prison. In January 1794 Citizeness Beauharnais had obtained her certificate of citizenship at Croissy. On her return to Paris she learned of the arrest of her sister-in-law, Marie-Françoise Beauharnais, wife of Alexandre's elder brother François, who had emigrated. She sought an audience with Vadier, the president of the Committee of Public Safety, who did not receive her personally but appointed a colleague to deputize for him. Sensing her husband was in danger, she wrote to Vadier:

"Your colleague made me appreciate your upright and virtuous patriotism and your constant interest – despite your doubts about the public-spiritedness of the *ci-devants* [former nobility], in the unfortunate victims of misunderstanding. I feel sure that in reading the petition you will take into consideration the state of a woman [Marie-Françoise Beauharnais] who is unhappy, but only because she used to belong to one of the enemies of the Republic, Beauharnais the Elder, whom you are acquainted with and who at the Constituent Assembly was in opposition to Alexandre, your colleague and my husband. I should be most grieved, Citizen Representative, if you were to confuse Alexandre with Beauharnais the Elder.

I put myself in your place: you must have doubts about the patriotism of the *ci-devants*, but it is not impossible that some of them may be fervent friends of Liberty and Equality. Alexandre has never deviated from these principles: he has constantly marched along their lines. Were he not a Republican, he would have gained neither my esteem nor my friendship. I am an American and he is the only member of that family I know; had I been permitted to see you, I would have dispelled your doubts. My house is a Republican one; before the Revolution my children were no different from the *sans-culottes* and I hope they will be worthy of the Republic. I write to you with frankness, as a *sans-culotte* of the Mountain [Robespierre's extreme party].

I, like you, do not believe in patriotism without uprightness or virtue; my only complaint about

your strictness is that it prevented me from seeing
you and having a brief talk with you. I ask no
favours of you, but I appeal to your sensitivity
and humanity on behalf of an unhappy
citizeness. If I have been deceived in what I have
been told of her position, and if she were, or
seems to you to be, suspicious, pray take no
notice of what I say, because – like you – I am
inexorable; but do not confuse your old colleague
with his brother; believe him worthy of your
esteem. Despite your refusal, I applaud your
strictness, in so far as it concerns myself, but I
cannot applaud the doubts you entertain about
my husband. 28th Nivôse of Year II [17 January
1794].''

Rosa Collina fastigiata

The warrant for the arrest of
'Beauharnais, formerly Commander-
in-Chief of the Army of the Rhine'
was dated 12th Ventôse (2 March)
and signed by Vadier and, among
others, the painter Jacques-Louis David. It was
followed not long after by a warrant for the arrest
of 'Citizeness Beauharnais, wife of the *ci-devant*
general', dated 30th Germinal (19 April).
Hortense recalled

''. . . the despair when one morning we learned
that my mother had come to kiss us, weeping,
and had left us, not wishing to wake us. 'Let them
sleep,' she told our governess. 'I could not endure
their tears. I would no longer have the strength to
leave them.' Waking up was dreadful. We were
suddenly alone, deprived at once of both our
father and our mother. It was the first tragedy of
my life.''

Rosa Indica Pumila

Rosa Alpina pendulina

On 19 Floréal (8 May 1794) Hortense and Eugène sent a petition to the National Convention, imploring them to let their mother go.

"Innocent children appeal to you, Citizen Representatives, for the freedom of their beloved mother who can be blamed for nothing but the misfortune of having entered a class to which she has shown herself a stranger, since she has never associated with any but the best patriots, the most excellent members of the Mountain. . . . Citizen Representatives, you will not permit the oppression of innocence, patriotism and virtue. Give back life to these unfortunate children, whose age is not fit for sadness."

They were both held in the Carmes prison. The Vicomtesse de Beauharnais shared a cell with the Duchesse d'Aiguillon and the Comtesse de Custine. The poet and statesman Lamartine would later write of it:

"It was a place where the September assassins [2–7 September 1792] had massacred most of the priests. Two of the slaughterers, tired of assassinations, were momentarily resting and had propped their sabres against the wall, to get their strength back. The silhouette of the two sabres, from the hilt up to the tip of the blade, had left an imprint of blood on the damp wall, drawing upon it a picture resembling those swords of fire brandished by the exterminating angels around the tabernacles. . . . Never had youth, beauty, and death been joined in so bloody a picture."

Rosa Bifera officinalis

Rosa Moschata flore semi-pleno

Rosa Cinnamomea Maialis

ortense later wrote in her memoirs:

"One day a woman whom we did not know came to our house to take my brother and me away with her, without any explanation. Mlle Lannoy [their governess] would not allow it, but the woman then produced a note of authorization in my mother's handwriting. My governess still hesitated, fearing some deception. Finally she surrendered. The woman took us to the Rue de Sèvres, to the bottom of a garden. Mysteriously, she made us go up into the gardener's house, warning us to keep very still. Opposite there was a large building. One of its windows opened, and my mother and father appeared. Surprised and excited, I cried out to my parents, reaching out for them; they motioned me to be silent, but a guard at the foot of the wall had heard us and began to raise the alarm. The unknown woman hurriedly took us away. We later learned that the window had been mercilessly walled up. It was the last time I saw my father. A few days later he no longer existed."

Rosa Andegavensis

lexandre Beauharnais was moved to the Conciergerie to stand trial. From there he wrote this last letter to his wife:

"4th Thermidor, Year II of the French Republic, one and indivisible [22 July 1794]. It would seem, from that mock interrogation to which several prisoners have been subjected today, that I have been a victim of the villainous slander of various aristocrats from this establishment, who profess to be patriots. Since I presume that these infernal machinations will follow me all the way to the revolutionary tribunal, I will have no hope of seeing you again, my friend, nor of holding my beloved children. I will not tell you of my regrets: my tender love for them, the fraternal attachment that binds me to you can leave you in no doubt as to the frame of mind with which I depart this world.

I am also full of regrets for the country I am leaving, for whom I would have given my life a thousand times over and whom I will no longer be able to serve, and who will see me slip away from her thinking me a bad citizen. This unbearable notion prevents me from asking you to guard my memory. Strive to re-establish it, proving that a whole lifetime devoted to the service of one's country and to the triumph of justice and equality must, in the eyes of the people, chase away those hateful slanderers, who have themselves been placed above suspicion.

This task will have to be postponed, however, because during the storms of revolution a great country which is fighting to break loose from its shackles must needs be imbued with a certain diffidence, and is more afraid of forgetting a guilty man than of accusing one who is innocent. I will die peacefully, however, my turmoil alleviated by the thought of my loved ones, but with the courage that characterizes the free man, a pure conscience and an honest soul, whose most fervent hopes are for the prosperity of the Republic. Farewell, my friend. Take consolation in our children, and console them by enlightening them and most of all by teaching them that they must blot out the memory of my torture through virtue and public-spiritedness, and remember rather my service and my titles to the national gratitude. Farewell. You are acquainted with all those whom I love. Console them, and by ministering to them, let my life be prolonged in their hearts. Farewell. I hold you, as I do my dear children, for the last time in my life, to my heart."

Rosa Rubiginosa Cretica

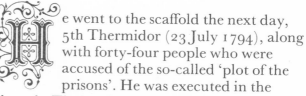

He went to the scaffold the next day, 5th Thermidor (23 July 1794), along with forty-four people who were accused of the so-called 'plot of the prisons'. He was executed in the Place du Thrône Renversé. His wife heard the news in the Carmes prison on 9th Thermidor (27 July). That same evening, a woman outside the prison windows performed a strange pantomime, waving her gown (*robe* in French), lifting up a stone (*pierre* – hence Robespierre), and drawing a finger across her neck, thus intimating the fall of the Incorruptible. The Terror was at an end.

Citizeness Beauharnais left prison on 19th Thermidor (6 August). While she was in prison Josephine had met and fallen in love with General Lazare Louis Hoche. Hoche, the son of one of the King's stablemen, had risen rapidly in the army and made brigadier-general at the age of twenty-five. He had been transferred to the Conciergerie where – mercifully for him – he had been forgotten about, and had then been freed two days previously.

Rosa Damascena Variegata

Rosa Rubiginosa Zabeth

It was an era of soldiers, an era of wars. Josephine was born just as the Seven Years War was concluded by the Peace of Paris. There followed fifteen years of peace, then in 1778 France clashed with the British again over the independence of the American colonies. This war lasted until the Treaty of Versailles in 1783. Nine years later, on 20 April 1792, under pressure from the Girondins, Louis XVI declared war on the 'King of Bohemia and Hungary', the Hapsburg Emperor. This triggered off the Revolutionary Wars which developed into the Napoleonic Wars, fought sometimes against one particular European power, sometimes against all of them. Generations later schoolchildren would get confused over just how many coalitions there had been. The only period of overall tranquillity occurred just after the peace of Amiens of 25 March 1803, but this was at an end by the summer of the following year.

There followed eleven more years of war. When Josephine died Napoleon had been defeated, but the Congress of Vienna had not yet been convened. The Hundred Days and Waterloo were still to take place before the Austrian Chancellor Metternich's lasting peace. Of the fifty years of Josephine's life, twenty-five, includ-

ing most of her childhood, were characterized by peace, and as many were set in the context of war.

Her life was acted out against a military backcloth. Her father was in charge of Martinique's coastal batteries shortly before her birth. Her first husband was a professional soldier whose service began under the King and ended abruptly on the guillotine under the Republic. Her father-in-law had forged a naval career which was more bureaucratic than bellicose. Her son fought with Napoleon during the Italian campaign, having already tasted the flavour of military life at the age of fourteen when he followed Hoche to the battlefield. Her second husband's connection with the military goes without saying, and even among the many lovers attributed to her the majority carried sabres and wore epaulettes.

Josephine was always surrounded by magnificent uniforms but also by echoes of the battlefield in all its horror. After the bloody Battle of Eylau, fought on 8 February 1807, Napoleon wrote to her:

"My friend, I am still in Eylau. Dead and wounded are strewn everywhere. This is the ugly side of war. One suffers, and the soul is weighed down at the sight of so many victims. . . ."

*S*oudain la scène change : au lieu de la gaiété,
C'est la mélancolie et la tranquillité,
C'est le calme imposant des lieux où sont nourries
La méditation, les longues rêveries.
Là, l'homme avec son coeur revient s'entretenir,
Médite le présent, plonge dans l'avenir,
Songe aux biens, songe aux maux épars dans sa carrière ;
Quelquefois, rejettant ses regards en arrière,
Se plaît a distinguer dans le cercle des jours
Ce peu d'instans, hélas ! et si chers et si courts,
Ces fleurs dans un désert, ces tems où le ramène
Le regret du bonheur, et de la peine.

The scene quick changes. Cheerfulness away!
Here pensive Melancholy shuns the day;
Impressive stillness every spot pervades,
And Grief and Meditation haunt the shades.
Here Man to commune with his heart retires,
And of the future and the past enquires;
Thinks on the good and ill the Gods bestow,
Of prosperous guilt, and undeserved woe;
And oft reverts, and mid the circling hours,
As blown in desert waste some scattered flowers,
Recalls those moments, short, alas! but dear,
Marked by past bliss, now blotted with a tear.

From Delille, *Les Jardins*, IV

Thermidor :
The Widow Beauharnais

1794–1796

Rosa Indica cruenta

Rosa Orbessanea

Rosa Rubiginosa memoralis

he historian and politician Thiers, in his famous *History of the French Revolution*, characterized the mid-1790s thus:

"Women contrived to give their attire an ancient appearance, as was the fashion of the time, and which was copied from [the painter] David. They had long since forsaken powder and crinolines. They wore bands round their hair, and the style of their garments was as close as possible to the simple tunic worn by women in Ancient Greece. Instead of high-heeled shoes they wore the shoes we see on ancient statues – a thin sole tied to the leg with ribbons. Young men with small black collars filled the auditorium of the Théâtre Feydeau and would occasionally give an ovation to the elegant, unusually dressed women who graced such gatherings with their presence.

Mme Tallien was the most beautiful and admired of all those women who introduced the new fashion; her salon was the most sparkling, and the most popular. The daughter of the Spanish banker Cabarrus, wife of a president at Bordèaux and recently re-married, to [the statesman] Tallien, she was partial to the company of men from both the Old and the New Régimes. She had rebelled against the Terror out of resentment as well as goodness. She wanted to invest her husband with the role of peacemaker and restorer of the evil perpetrated by the Revolution. She gathered around her in her house all those who, with him, had contributed to 9th Thermidor, and sought to conquer them by flattering them, persuading them to strive for public recognition, and making them hope that they might forget their past – which was essential for many of them. She further instilled into them faith in the power that was now promised to the adversaries, rather than to the partisans of the Terror.

She surrounded herself with charming women who contributed to this forgivable exercise of seduction. Among these stood out the widow of the unfortunate General Alexandre Beauharnais, a young Creole who was attractive not so much on account of her beauty but rather because of her extreme grace.

To these gatherings were summoned those simple men who were passionately devoted to their cause and who had had a hard and tormented life. They were caressed, and sometimes teased about their clothes, their manners and their rigorous principles. They were made to take their place at table next to men they would formerly have persecuted as aristocrats, wealthy speculators and squanderers of the public fortune. They were thus forced to be aware of their inferiority."

osephine wrote to her mother, with family news, on 30th Brumaire of Year III of the Republic (20 November 1794):

"Someone leaving for New England has promised to forward this letter to you. I am so happy that it will enable you to know that your daughter and grandchildren are well. You will no doubt have learned of the tragedy that has befallen me: I have been a widow these four months past. The only consolation and support that are left to me are my children and yourself, mother dear."

To her aunt, Mme Renaudin, she wrote about the Tallien *salon*:

"Mme Tallien is immensely beautiful and kind. She draws on her extensive influence only to grant favours to those unfortunate people who appeal to her, and to everything she concedes she brings such an expression of satisfaction that you might believe it were she who owed you thanks. Her friendship towards me is warm and tender. Mine, I can assure you, is similar to the friendship I feel for you. You may thus imagine my feelings towards Mme Tallien."

And signing herself 'the widow Beauharnais' she corresponded with Barras, one of the most powerful men of the moment, whom she had earlier known slightly:

"It has been a long time since I have had the pleasure of seeing you. It is remiss of you to forsake an old acquaintance like this. I trust you will respond to this reprimand. I now reside at No. 371, Rue de l'Université."

Rosa Gallica Purpurea Velutina, Parva

Rosa Sempervirens globosa

O n 13th Vendémiaire (5 October 1795) the twenty-six-year-old General Napoleon Bonaparte, who was in Paris in search of a command, found his chance to acquire one. The Parisian sections were planning a protest against the National Convention. Barras summoned the young general and gave him three minutes in which to agree to the position of second-in-command. He accepted. As General Baron Thiébault recalled:

"I can still see his hat, on which perched a casual feather that had not been very well affixed. His tricoloured sash was knotted carelessly, his clothes were badly cut and the sword he carried scarcely seemed the weapon that was to make his fortune."

Joachim Murat, squadron commander of the 21st Cavalry Division, together with his three hundred men one night impounded some forty cannon at the Champ des Sablons. Bonaparte disposed them as he knew how. As he wrote to his brother Joseph:

"The Convention appointed Barras to command the armed forces of the Government: the committee chose me as second-in-command. We disposed our troops. The enemy attacked us at the Tuileries. We killed a large number of them. They killed thirty of our men, and wounded sixty. We have disarmed the sections, and all is quiet. As usual, I haven't a scratch."

On 16 October he was promoted to lieutenant-general, and on the twenty-sixth he was commander of the Army of the Interior.

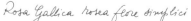
Rosa Gallica rosea flore simplici

Rosa alba flore pleno

At about this time Napoleon met the widowed Josephine de Beauharnais. Her son Eugène wrote:

"I myself was the cause of his first meeting with my mother. Following 13th Vendémiaire Parisian citizens were forbidden, under penalty of death, to possess weapons. I could not resign myself to being separated from the sword my father had carried, and which had seen such honourable and dazzling service. I hoped to obtain permission to keep that sword, and took steps to do so by approaching General Bonaparte. The meeting he granted me was all the more moving because it awoke in me the memory of my still recent loss. My sensitivity in this matter, coupled with some felicitous answers I gave the General, made him interested in meeting my family, and the following day he came in person to bring me the authorization I had so ardently wished for. He asked if he might visit us again, and seemed to enjoy my mother's company more and more."

On 6th Brumaire (28 October 1795) Josephine addressed a letter to General Napoleon Bonaparte:

"You no longer come to visit a friend who is fond of you. You have utterly abandoned her. It is wrong of you to do so, because she is very attached to you. Come to luncheon with me a week tomorrow. I need to see you and talk of your interests with you. Goodnight, my friend. I embrace you."

Rosa Centifolia Caryophyllea

Rosa Turbinata

About Barras, with whom Josephine had recently renewed her earlier acquaintance, we have this information from contemporary memoirs:

"One of our neighbours at Croissy was Mme de Beauharnais, whose future great fortune we could not foresee at that time. She only returned occasionally, once a week, in order to receive Barras and the many people that formed his entourage. In the morning we would see baskets of provisions being delivered, then *gendarmes* on horseback would fill the road from Nanterre to Croissy, because more often than not the young Director would arrive on horseback. Mme de Beauharnais's house, as is the Creole custom, was somewhat luxurious in its decoration. . . . Poultry, game and exotic fruit cluttered the kitchen – we ourselves were then in direst poverty – but there were no pans, glasses or plates, which they invariably had to borrow from us."

Rosa Indica subviolacea

Rosa sepium rosea

Rosa Indica Pumila
(flore simplici)

arras is the most malicious witness of all those who reconstruct the legend of the Creole girl who became an Empress. As he recalled in his memoirs:

"[Bonaparte] had noticed among the gentlewomen who called most frequently on me at the Luxembourg the widow Beauharnais, a woman of rather gentle manners, most kindly, and who occasionally conversed with me in more private fashion than the others did. Mme Beauharnais was reputed to have some influence with me – some there were who believed she had been my mistress, others that she still was. What is, however, certain, is that she had been the mistress of General Hoche, *e di tutti quanti* [and indeed of everyone else]. Not that she did not love General Hoche in preference to the others; this is easily imagined. He was our best soldier, and one of our handsomest men.

Whether from motives of ambition rather than love, since she deceived him like the rest, Mme Beauharnais had pushed her pretensions on Hoche so far as to want him to obtain a divorce so that she might marry him. But a feeling of tender esteem bound Hoche to his young and virtuous spouse. He had perhaps neglected his duties as a husband, but he had not forsaken her just for a passing gallantry, such as the one born of his chance meeting with Mme Beauharnais in prison. He had consequently repulsed with horror this suggestion of divorce, telling Mme Beauharnais in no uncertain terms that a man might temporarily indulge in having a whore as his mistress, but it was no reason to marry her. . . .

I must in this connection point out a distinction which the acquaintances of Mme Tallien and Mme Beauharnais agreed in establishing between these two gentlewomen. . . . The liaisons of Mme Tallien were for her genuine enjoyment, and she brought to them all the ardour and passion of her temperament. As for Mme Beauharnais, it was the general belief that her relationships, even with the men whose physical advantages she best appreciated, were not as generous as those of Mme Tallien. Even though physical attraction appeared to be the cause of Mme Beauharnais' *affaires*, her libertinism sprang merely from the mind, while her heart played no part in the pleasures of her body. In brief, never loving except from motives

Rosa Malmundariensis

of interest, the lewd Creole never lost sight of business, although those possessing her might suppose she was conquered by them and had freely given herself."

ortense recalled a dinner party she attended at Barras's:

"My mother had only been able to part from my brother and myself by making us return to Paris on frequent visits. During one of those visits she announced that she was about to go to dinner at Barras's, and that we were to accompany her.

'How could you, mother!' I exclaimed emotionally. 'Consorting with those people! Have you forgotten all the tragedies that have befallen our family?'

'My dear daughter,' she replied, with her usual unwavering tenderness, 'since your father's death I have been constantly engaged in reclaiming what remains of his fortune, which we had thought lost to us. Don't you think I owe some gratitude to those who have helped and protected me?'

I sensed my error. I apologized and followed my mother to the Directory, which had been established at the Luxembourg Palace. Barras had gathered numerous guests round him. Tallien and his wife were the only people I knew. At the table [the date of this meal was 1st Pluviôse, 21 January 1796, and the occasion the third anniversary of Louis XVI's execution] I sat between my mother and a general who, in order to talk to her, annoyed me by lunging forward with such excitement and perseverance that I had to sit farther back. I could thus observe, in spite of myself, that he was handsome, with a very expressive countenance, but strikingly pale. His tone was fiery, and he seemed interested only in my mother. It was General Bonaparte."

General Marmont wrote about this meeting:

Rosa Indica

Rosa Banksiae

Rosa Indica

my inmost self, when I quaff from your lips and from your heart a scorching flame? Yes! One night has taught me how far your portrait falls short of yourself! You start at midday: in three hours I shall see you again. Till then, a thousand kisses, *mio dolce amor*: but give me none back, for they set my blood on fire."

Years later Mme de Rémusat asked Josephine about Napoleon at this time, and recorded her response in her memoirs.

"When I questioned her as to what Bonaparte was like in his youth, she told me that he was then dreamy, silent, and awkward in the society of women, but passionate and fascinating, although rather an odd person in every way. She blamed the campaign in Egypt for having changed his temper, and developed that petty despotism from which she afterwards suffered so much."

Rosa Damascena aurora

"General Bonaparte had fallen in love with Mme Beauharnais in the fullest sense of the term. It was, by all accounts, his first great passion and he embraced it with all the energy he possessed."

he passion observed by Marmont was expressed in vivid terms in a letter sent formally from General Bonaparte to Citizeness Beauharnais:

"I awake all filled with you. Your image, and the intoxicating pleasures of last night, allow my senses no rest. Sweet and matchless Josephine, how strangely you work upon my heart! Are you angry with me? Are you unhappy? Are you upset? . . . My soul is broken with grief, and my love for you forbids repose. But how can I rest any more, when I yield to the feeling that masters

Rosa Rapa

Rosa Pimpinellifolia rubra
(Flore multiplici)

laire-Elizabeth-Jeanne Gravier de Vergennes, the Comtesse de Rémusat, came from a family with which the Vicomtesse de Beauharnais had become acquainted at Croissy, on her return from Martinique. She had been Hortense's closest childhood friend, since she was only three years older than Josephine's daughter. During the Empire she was lady-in-waiting and confidante to Josephine. Her observations are always acute:

"Being a friend of the beautiful Mme Tallien, she was introduced into the society of the Directory, and was especially favoured by Barras. Mme de Beauharnais had very little fortune, and her taste for clothes and luxury rendered her dependent on those who could help her indulge it. Without being precisely pretty, she possessed many personal charms. Her features were delicate, her expression was sweet. Her mouth was very small, and concealed her bad teeth. Her complexion was rather dark, but with the help of skilfully applied red and white she remedied that defect. Her figure was perfect, and her limbs were flexible and delicate – her movements were easy and elegant. La Fontaine's line could not have been more aptly applied than to her: '*Et la grâce, plus belle encore que la beauté*' [And grace more beautiful than beauty].

She dressed with perfect taste, enhancing the beauty of what she wore. With these advantages and the constant care bestowed upon her attire, she contrived not to be eclipsed by the youth and beauty of many of the women by whom she was surrounded.

To all this, as I have already said, she added extreme kindness of heart, a remarkably even

Rosa Gallica Regalis

Rosa Leucantha

temper, and great readiness to forget any wrong that had been done to her.

She was not a person of remarkable intellect. A Creole, and frivolous, her education had been a good deal neglected; but she was aware of her deficiencies and never made blunders in conversation. She possessed true natural tact; she readily found pleasant things to say: her memory was good – a useful quality for those in high position. Unhappily, she was deficient in depth of feeling and elevation of mind. She preferred to charm her husband by her beauty, rather than by the influence of certain virtues. She carried complaisance to excess for his sake, and kept her hold on him by concessions which, perhaps, contributed to increase the contempt with which he habitually regarded women. She might have taught him some useful lessons; but she feared him, and allowed him to dictate to her in

everything. She was fickle, easy to move and easy to appease, incapable of lasting feeling, of sustained attention, of serious reflection, and although her greatness did not turn her head, neither did it educate her. The bent of her character led her to be compassionate to the unfortunate; but she could only dwell on the troubles of individuals – she did not think of the woes of France. The genius of Bonaparte overawed her: she criticized him only in what concerned her personally; in everything else she respected what he called 'the force of his destiny'. He exerted an evil influence over her, for he inspired her with contempt for morality, with a large share of his own characteristic suspicion, and he taught her the art of lying, which they both practised with skill and effect.''

he marriage banns between Josephine and Napoleon were posted on 20th Pluviôse (18 February 1796). On 12th Ventôse (2 March) General Bonaparte was made commander of the army in Italy by the Directory. General Baron Thiébault commented: 'The public saw in this posting favour for Mme Bonaparte rather than wisdom and concern for France's interests.' In the words of Lucien Bonaparte: 'Barras has taken charge of Josephine's dowry, which is the chief command of the army in Italy.' Marmont observed: 'I would be tempted to think that he [Napoleon] thought that with this marriage he was taking a higher step up the social ladder than when, sixteen years later, he shared his bed with "Caesar's wife" [Marie-Louise of Austria].'

Rosa Alpina flore variegato

osephine's suspicion and jealousy, even at this time, are revealed in this letter to her from General Bonaparte:

"Nine in the morning. I left you with a heavy heart. I went to bed extremely irritable. I should have thought that the esteem in which you hold me would have banished from your mind the worry that was tormenting you last night. If this care were to take over your spirit, you would be extremely unfair, madame, and I would be very unhappy. How could you think that I do not love you for yourself!!! And for what else then, pray? Do you suppose I have changed so much? How could a soul so pure conceive of so base a notion? It still astonishes me, even more than the notion itself, which on my awakening this morning brings me helplessly and without rancour to your feet. No man could be weaker or more degraded, that is sure. What then is your strange power, matchless Josephine? One of your thoughts poisons my entire life, torments my soul with the most conflicting emotions, but a stronger feeling and a gentler mood assail me and bring me guiltily back to you. I am well aware that if we argue, I should deny my heart and my conscience, but you have seduced them both – they still belong to you. Have you slept well, *mio dolce amor*? You have only thought of me twice. I kiss you three times, once on your heart, once on your mouth and once on your eyes."

Rosa aciphylla

he marriage took place on 19th Ventôse (9 March 1796) in the town hall of the 11th *arrondissement*, in Rue d'Antin. Citizeness Beauharnais, who was thirty-three, declared that she was twenty-eight. General Bonaparte also gave his age as twenty-eight, although he was really only twenty-six. One of the witnesses was under age; the others included Tallien for the bride and Barras for the bridegroom. The bride ceased to call herself Rose, as she had done until then, and called herself Josephine, while her husband became officially Bonaparte instead of Buonaparte.

The couple went to the house in Rue Chantereine which Citizeness Beauharnais had rented in the summer of 1795. During the night there was an incident involving Fortuné, Josephine's dog. Bonaparte later related the story:

"See that young upstart? He's my rival. He was in complete possession of Madame's bed when I married her. I tried to get him out of the room, a vain enterprise. I was told that one either had to sleep elsewhere or consent to the arrangement. This irked me somewhat, but I had to take it or leave it. I gave in. The pet was less accommodating than I; I bear evidence of that on my knee."

On the evening of 21st Ventôse (11 March 1796), General Bonaparte left for Italy.

Rosa Pomponia flore sublimplici

Rosa Tomentosa

55

Josephine was always immaculately elegant. 'The best taste and the most perfect conception of elegance always governed her wardrobe,' wrote Bausset, prefect of the imperial palace. 'Her clothes always made her seem younger than she was.' Revolution in political terms was – not for the first or last time – reflected by revolution in fashion. After the Jacobin Terror was over a new image was dreamed up for women, along the lines of David's Grecian style, now that the Revolution had swept away the Rococo elegance of both the court and the aristocracy. Josephine, together with Thérésia Cabarrus and Mme Tallien, was an ardent follower of the new style.

Bare shoulders, bare arms and side slits were its chief features. Clothes were feather-light and women caught cold and died of pneumonia. At a reception given by Barras, Mme Tallien wagered that all the clothing she wore – dress, bracelets and Grecian sandals – weighed no more than two six-franc pieces. The scales were brought, Mme Tallien removed all her clothing – to the delight of a few dozen guests – and won the wager. With the Empire, which introduced a certain bourgeois morality, Napoleon had all fireplaces walled up, so that fires could not be lit and women would thus be forced to wear heavier clothing. This also had the effect of stimulating the national textile industry.

Josephine became the uneclipsed arbiter of fashion under the Consulate and the Empire. The Austrian Marie-Louise may have taken her place in the imperial bed but she did not leave the same imprint on fashion. When Josephine died at Malmaison, having left court five years earlier, an inventory of her wardrobe listed 47 shawls and 9 cashmere gowns; 211 gowns of silk, crêpe, muslin, tulle, velvet and satin; 223 lawn chemises and 104 muslin ones; 158 pairs of stockings in silk, plain cotton and embroidered cotton . . . and so on.

Court gown with train and floral decoration, 1802. The great dressmaker of the Revolution and the Empire *was Leroy, a man of the ancien régime, dressmaker to Marie Antoinette, and who at the beginning of the* *Revolution still dressed in pink satin.*

Left to right: House gown with bonnet trimmed with tulle, and a little shawl around the shoulders, 1809; Empire fashions with high-waisted gowns, puff sleeves, little bonnets and gloves covering the elbow, 1808.

Left: Demi-parure, or semi-formal gown, with asymmetrical parasol, from Year XI (1803).
Right: Ceremonial clothes, with a straw bonnet for the lady and a plumed hat and sword for the gentleman. Leroy was instructed by the Convention to design a costume worthy of the Revolution. He produced a tricoloured creation with 'Liberty, Equality, Fraternity' embroidered on it. During the Empire he dressed Josephine, Paulette and Caroline Bonaparte, and Marie Walewska. After the restoration of the monarchy his clients included Princess Metternich, the Duchess of Wellington and Princess Talleyrand.

Ce n'est plus du château la parure stérile,
La grace inanimée et la pompe immobile :
Tout vit, tout est peuplé dans ces murs, sous ces toîts.
Que d'oiseaux différens et d'instinct et de voix,
Habitans sous l'ardoise, ou la tuile, ou le chaume,
Famille, nation, république, royaume,
M'occupent de leurs moeurs, m'amusent de leurs jeux !
A leur tête est le coq, père, amant, chef heureux,
Qui, roi sans tyrannie, et sultan sans mollesse,
A son serrail ailé prodiguant sa tendresse,
Aux droits de la valeur joint ceux de la beauté,
Commande avec douceur, caresse avec fierté,
En fait pour les plaisirs, et l'empire, et la gloire,
Aime, combat, triumphe, et chante sa victoire.

Unlike the splendid mansion, doomed by Fate
To pomp inanimate, and barren state,
With life and motion teems the rustic bound;
Here birds of various voice and kind are found,
Kingdoms and states in social bond allied,
Who under thatch, and tile, and slate reside.
Bold at their head struts gallant Chanticleer,
In pride of plumage, and unknown to fear;
In him the father, lover, warrior see,
A king, a sultan from injustice free,
Who, famed for valour and for beauty, proves
His flame impartial to his feathered loves,
Rules without tyranny, and fond, though proud,
Fights, conquers, loves, and chants his feats aloud.

From Delille, *Les Jardins*, IV

58

Madame Bonaparte

1796–1804

Rosa Bifera alba

After conquering Italy in 1796 Napoleon wrote to Josephine with a soldier's impatience, first from Nice on 10th Germinal (31 March):

"Not a day passes without my loving you, not a night but I hold you in my arms. I cannot drink a cup of tea without cursing the martial ambition that separates me from the soul of my life. Whether I am buried in business, or leading my troops, or inspecting the camps, my adorable Josephine fills my mind, takes up all my thoughts, and reigns alone in my heart. If I am torn from you with the swiftness of the rushing Rhône, it is that I may see you again the sooner. If I rise to work at midnight, it is to put forward by a few days my darling's arrival. And yet, in your letter of the twenty-third, and again of 26th Ventôse, you call me [the formal term] '*vous*!' '*Vous*' yourself! Wretch! How could you ever write such a letter?"

And again from Carrù, on 5th Floréal (24 April):

"Your letters light up my days, and my happy days are few. Junot is taking twenty-two soldiers to Paris. You must come back with him, do you understand? If this cannot be, then he need not return at all. It would be an irreparable calamity, an inconsolable sorrow and constant suffering for me if I were unfortunate enough to see him come back alone, my adorable friend. He will see you, he will bask in your temple; perhaps you will grant him the unique and priceless favour of kissing your cheek, and I shall be alone, and so very far away. But you will come, won't you? You will be by my side, against my heart, in my arms, your lips against mine. Spread your wings and come to me, come to me! . . ."

From Milan, on 4th Prairial (23 May):

"There has been a large reception here; five or six hundred pretty and elegant young ladies sought to please me, but none of them resembled you; none of them had those sweet, harmonious features that are so well engraved on my heart. I saw no one but you, thought of no one but you. . . ."

Rosa Rubiginosa flore Semipleno

Rosa Geminata

From Tortona, on 24th Prairial (14 June):

"I thought you had arrived in Milan. As soon as
I had left the battlefield at Borghetto, I ran to
look for you; I could not find you! Some days
later, a messenger informed me you had not set
off on your journey, and brought me no letters
from you. My soul was rent asunder by pain. I
thought myself abandoned by everything I hold
dear on this earth. Throughout my life my
emotions have never been anything less than
passionate. Ravaged by sorrow, I may have
written to you in a tone that was too strong. If my
letters have distressed you, I shall be inconsolable
for the rest of my life. . . . Since the Ticino has
overflowed, I have come here to Tortona to wait
for you. Every day I waited in vain for you three
leagues away; finally, four hours ago, I was still
there. I see a letter arriving telling me quite
simply that you are not coming. . . ."

Still at Tortona, on 27th Prairial (15 June):

"My life is a complete nightmare. A deadly
premonition chokes me. I am no longer alive; I
have lost more than my life, more than
happiness, more than peace of mind; I am almost
without hope. I have sent a messenger to you. He
will remain in Paris just four hours, and will
bring me back your answer. Write ten pages; this
is the only thing that will console me a little. . . ."

And from Pistoia, on 8th Messidor (26 June):

"In a month my good friend has only sent me two
notes, each a mere three lines long. Is she busy?
Does she not feel the need to write to her good
friend? Let alone think of him. . . . For your
husband, to live without thinking of Josephine
would be the same as not existing at all, would be
death. The image of you soothes my thoughts
and gladdens the dark and sinister melancholy
and pain I am beset with. Perhaps one day I shall
see you. . . ."

The day he had so longed for came on 13 July.
They met in Milan, at the Serbelloni Palace.

Rosa Gallica flore marmoreo

Rosa Dumetorum

Josephine had left for Italy with Junot, Joseph Bonaparte, Hamelin (a businessman who had lent her money and who was expecting commissions for military supplies) and others, including the twenty-five-year-old Hippolyte Charles, a great raconteur renowned for his witty aphorisms and, it was rumoured, Josephine's lover. The Parisians had already hailed her as 'Notre Dame des Victoires' (Our Lady of Victories). General Bonaparte, wrote Mme de Rémusat,

". . . sometimes left her with the rearguard of the army, until a victory had secured the safety of the road. . . . How strange it must have been for a woman to find herself one of the moving powers of the triumphant march of an army, at a time when politics alone governed the actions of men!"

On the eve of one of his great battles, Bonaparte wrote to her:

"Here I am, far away from you! I seem to have fallen into the deepest darkness. I need the deadly clarity of the thunderbolts I shall release on the enemy to come out of the darkness wherein I have been plunged by your absence. Josephine, you were crying when I left you. Crying! The thought of this makes my whole being quiver with rage. Calm yourself. Würmser [the Austrian commander who surrendered at Mantua in 1797] will pay dearly for those tears I saw you shed."

In September 1796 Josephine wrote to her aunt, who had finally married the Marquis de la Ferté-Beauharnais about her triumphs in Italy:

"Signor Serbelloni will tell you, dear aunt, of my reception in Italy, and how I have been fêted everywhere I have travelled through; all the princes of Italy give parties in my honour, even the Archduke of Tuscany, the Emperor's brother. Well, I prefer to be simply a private person in France. I do not favour the honours bestowed on me by this country! If happiness were to bear the fruit of good health, then I should be more than healthy. I have the most agreeable husband in

the world. I want for nothing. My wishes are his wishes. He worships me all day long as though I were a deity; it would be impossible to be a better husband than he is."

But it palled soon enough. To her daughter Hortense she wrote in February 1797:

"I am well, my dear Hortense. For six days now I have had no more fever. I was a little unwell in Bologna; and I am tired of Italy. In spite of all the parties in my honour and the pleasing reception the people of this country have given me, I cannot grow accustomed to such long separations from my dear children; I need to hold them close to my heart. But I have good reason to suppose that the moment when I can do so again is not very distant, and this helps me greatly in coping with the indisposition with which I have been afflicted."

During the summer the entire Bonaparte family gathered in the Villa Mombello, near Milan, for the wedding of Napoleon's sister Paulette and Leclerc. It was an impressive celebration with many dragoons, grenadiers, cavalrymen, hussars and diplomats. It was at Mombello that a mastiff killed Fortuné, Josephine's dog. Hippolyte Charles instantly supplied her with another. Some time afterwards the General ran into the cook, who was training a mastiff. The man was keeping the dog away from the villa, he said, because he was upset by Josephine's distress. 'Nonsense,' Bonaparte is said to have retorted, 'let him run where he wants. Perhaps he will get rid of this other one for me as well. . . .'

Rosa Pimpinellifolia flore variegato

Rosa Gallica agatha
(var. delphiniana)

Rosa Rubiginosa aculeatissima

Rosa Pimpinellifolia alba flore multiplici

63

Rosa Centifolia crenata

Rosa Pumila

ortense's memoirs tell us about the family's changed lifestyle as a result of Napoleon's successes.

"I had been at my grandfather's for a few days when General Bonaparte returned from Italy [5 December 1797]. All Paris reverberated with his name. Everyone wanted to see him and admire him. He went to my mother's house in Rue Chantereine, which was instantly renamed Rue de la Victoire. My grandfather took my cousin and me to see him one morning. What a change on our little house, which had once been so peaceful! It was full of generals and officers. The guards were having difficulty in keeping the impatient crowds and society people away, all of them eager to see the conqueror of Italy. Finally, despite the throngs of people, we reached the

general who was in the middle of luncheon, surrounded by numerous ministers. He greeted me with all the tenderness of a father, told me of my brother whom he had sent to Zante, Corfu, Cephalonia and Rome to spread the news of the peace, and he announced the imminent return of my mother. A few days later I was overjoyed to see her again, and to be able to go and live with her. She would often delight in telling me of her travels, and of the dangers she had encountered."

Rosa Villosa Terebenthina

Rosa Multiflora carnea

n 19 May 1798 General Bonaparte sailed from Toulon, bound for Egypt and further conquest. Later he wrote to his wife, saying he was sending the frigate *Pomona* to her so that she might join him, but on 1 August Nelson destroyed the French fleet in Aboukir Bay and all communications with France were cut.

The following year Josephine bought the house at Malmaison, on the banks of the Seine, not far from Paris. Mme de Rémusat wrote:

"It was at Malmaison that Mme Bonaparte showed us an immense quantity of pearls, diamonds, and cameos, which constituted the contents of her jewel-case. Even at that time it might have figured in a tale from the *Arabian Nights*, and it was destined to receive further rich acquisitions. Invaded and grateful Italy had

contributed, and so had the Pope as a mark of appreciation of the respect with which the conqueror treated him by denying himself the pleasure of planting his flag upon the walls of Rome. The reception rooms at Malmaison were sumptuously decorated with the spoils of Italy, and each of the generals who figured in the Italian campaign exhibited booty of the same kind."

Hippolyte Charles was never far away. Talleyrand wrote of this *affaire*:

"Without a care for her own position, she risked her husband's good name, and all for the sake of a dalliance with a man so bland, so smothered by the weight of his insignificance, that not even the impact of his liaison with the hero's wife could pluck him from the profound anonymity that enveloped him."

apoleon was not happy in Egypt. Eugène wrote in his memoirs:

"At that time the General-in-Chief began to feel very hurt, both because of the discontent that reigned throughout part of the army and because of the news from France, which attempted to shatter his domestic harmony. Although I was very young, I inspired a fair amount of trust in him. Pacing up and down in his tent, he would open his heart to me. I was the only one in whom he could confide openly. I tried to temper his resentment; I consoled him as best I could, and as much as my age and the respect in which I held him would let me."

Bonaparte had in fact learned the bad news of his wife's infidelity from two of his generals. He had called for a divorce – a public, scandalous divorce. Then he had written to his brother Joseph, while Eugène wrote to his mother. The British, however, intercepted both letters, which were then published in the newspapers. The

Rosa Inermis

Rosa Gallica caerule

Rosa Campanulata alba

British also disembarked Lieutenant Fourès of the 22nd Light Infantry Division in Egypt, having captured him at sea. Bonaparte had sent him back to France, with a view to taking his wife Pauline as his mistress.

Rosa Mollissima

Napoleon decided to return to France. Mme de Rémusat wrote in her memoirs that in October 1799

"... a rumour of Bonaparte's arrival at Fréjus arose. He came back with his mind full of the evil reports that Lucien [his brother] had repeated to him in his letters. His wife, on hearing of his disembarkation, set out to join him; she missed him, had to retrace her steps, and returned to their house in the Rue Chantereine some hours after his arrival there. She descended from her carriage in haste, followed by her son and daughter, and ran up the stairs leading to his room.

Imagine her surprise to find the door locked! She called to Bonaparte, and begged him to open it. He replied, through the door, that it should never again be opened for her. Then she wept, fell on her knees, implored him for her sake and that of her two children. But all in vain – the silence remained unbroken and several hours of the night passed in this dreadful suspense.

At last, however, moved by her sobs and her perseverance, Bonaparte opened the door at about four o'clock in the morning, and appeared, as Mme Bonaparte herself told me, with a stern countenance, which, however, betrayed that he too had been weeping. He bitterly reproached her with her conduct, her forgetfulness of him, all the real or imaginary sins of which Lucien had accused her, and concluded by announcing an eternal separation. Then he turned to Eugène Beauharnais, who was at that time about twenty.

'As for you,' he said, 'you shall not bear the burden of your mother's faults. You shall be always my son. I will keep you with me.'

'No, no, General,' replied Eugène. 'I must share the ill fortune of my mother, and from this moment I say farewell to you.'

These words shook Bonaparte's resolution. He opened his arms to Eugène, weeping. His wife and Hortense knelt at his feet and embraced his knees. And soon afterwards all was forgiven. In the explanation that ensued Mme Bonaparte succeeded in clearing herself from the accusations of her brother-in-law. Bonaparte, then burning to avenge her, sent for Lucien at seven o'clock in the morning and had him, without any forewarning, ushered into the room where the husband and wife, entirely reconciled, occupied the same bed."

As he would later tell Lucien, 'The warriors of Egypt are like those at the siege of Troy, and their wives have reserved for them the same kind of fidelity.'

Rosa longifolia

Rosa Alpina vulgaris

Laure Junot, the Duchesse d'Abrantès, described Josephine's new house:

"Malmaison, at the time I am speaking of, was a pretty country house with agreeable environs, as a residence, but very inconvenient and most unwholesome. Brunetière, who was somehow mixed up in the affair, told me that Mme Bonaparte had made this acquisition as a child buys a new doll that strikes her fancy, without considering whether it will long amuse her. The park was small, sloping on all sides, and resembled a pretty English garden. . . ."

Méneval, Bonaparte's secretary, wrote about the way of life of its new occupants:

"At Malmaison the First Consul [Bonaparte had assumed power less than four weeks after his return from Egypt, with the *coup d'état* of 18th Brumaire] spent whatever time was not taken up by study in the park, and even then he put his time to good use. Josephine spent her time as she wished. She received numerous friends during the day; she would take luncheon with some women friends and with acquaintances both old and new. She had no talent for agreeable pastimes; she did not draw, and she was no musician. There was a harp in her apartments, and she would play this when she had nothing better to do – always the same tune. She devoted much of her time to tapestry work, assisted by her ladies-in-waiting and her guests, and this is how she covered the furniture for the drawing-room at Malmaison. Napoleon approved of her being thus occupied."

The Duchesse d'Abrantès described how Napoleon liked playing games:

"When he was in good humour, the weather fine, and he had a few minutes' leisure from the labour which at that time was killing him, he would play at barriers with us. He cheated us at *reversis* [a card game], would throw us down, or come upon us without crying *barre*! but these tricks were only calculated to raise a laugh. His coat was on such occasions laid aside, and he ran like a hare, or rather like the gazelle, which he would feed with a boxful of tobacco, and tell to run after us, and the tormenting animal tore our clothes, and sometimes our legs."

he Marquise de la Tour du Pin mentioned a visit to the house which revealed something of Josephine's character.

"I went one morning to Malmaison. It was after the battle of Marengo. Mme Bonaparte received me extraordinarily well and after luncheon, which was set in a charming dining-room, she took me to visit her gallery. We were alone and she took advantage of this to give me the most boring accounts of the origins of the masterpieces and also of the collection of very fine small pictures standing on easels. It was the Pope who had insisted that she should accept that fine painting of the Albanian woman. Canova had given her *La Danseuse* and *Hebe*. The city of Milan had presented her with this and that. I was careful not to take these tales literally, but as I had a great admiration for the victor of Marengo, I should have preferred Mme Bonaparte to tell me the truth – that they had all been taken at the point of the sword. The good woman was an inveterate liar. Even when the plain truth would have been more interesting, or more striking than an invention, she preferred to invent."

Rosa Spinulifolia Sematratiana

Rosa Myriacantha

s a husband Napoleon could at times be capricious and even tyrannical. Bonaparte extended the property of Malmaison by buying the woods at Butard, and the Duchesse d'Abrantès recalled:

"As this was the first time of our going to Butard, the postillion did not know his way, and the road we followed brought us to a stream with banks so steep that the passage was a difficult one for a carriage. The moment Mme Bonaparte descried this precipice, as she called it, she forbade him to proceed a step further. Bonaparte, who was riding ahead, turned round.

'What is the matter?' he said. 'What is this new caprice about? . . . Come,' he said to the little lad who drove the carriage, 'a good plunge, then draw in the reins, and you are over.'

Mme Bonaparte uttered a piercing shriek, to which the forest re-echoed.

'You shall never keep me in the carriage! Let me out! Bonaparte! I entreat you in mercy! Let me out!'

Weeping, and clasping her hands, she was truly an object of pity. Napoleon looked at her, but far from relenting he shrugged his shoulders and roughly commanded her to be silent.

'It is absolute childishness. You shall pass, and in the carriage.'

The scene was protracted. Laure Junot was made to get down, as she was pregnant, and Bonaparte escorted her to the other side of the stream.

When we had crossed, Napoleon saw that the

Rosa canina nitens

Rosa multiflora platyphylla

carriage did not stir, for Josephine, crying as if her execution was being prepared, entreated the postillion to stay another minute, much as a condemned criminal would beg a reprieve.

'Very well, sir,' said the First Consul. 'Do you choose to obey my orders?'

It was not lightly that he applied a stroke of his whip to the postillion's back, who, instantly whipping both his horses, made them take the plunge. The carriage crossed the stream, but with such difficulty that one of the springs was broken and a pin loosened. Mme Bonaparte was still worse used. Her whole frame was shaking with pain, fear, and rage, and, conscious that such passions give an interesting expression only to young faces, she wrapped herself in a large muslin veil, and we only heard her sobs till our arrival at Butard. Her husband, incensed at finding her still in tears, pulled her almost brutally out of the carriage and dragged her a short distance to the wood. We could hear him scolding all the more angrily since he had set out prepared for a happy excursion.''

Rosa Candolleana Elegans

Rosa Centifolia Bipinnata

Rosa Rubiginosa anemoneflora

Rosa Eglanteria Luteola

After the *coup d'état* of 18th Brumaire the First Consul established himself at the Luxembourg Palace, formerly the seat of the Directory. After confirmation of the referendum he moved to the Tuileries, where Louis XVI and Marie Antoinette had lived before their execution.

'A sad place, General,' Count Roederer told Napoleon.

'Yes,' he replied. 'Like greatness.'

Josephine on the other hand complained to her daughter: 'I shall not be happy here. I feel a dreadful sense of foreboding whenever I enter this place.'

Laure Junot was presented at the Tuileries shortly after her marriage to General Junot and described the experience in her memoirs:

"Mme Bonaparte was in the same place which she then occupied as mistress of the house, and where afterwards she was seated as sovereign of the world. I found her before a tapestry frame working on a piece of canvas, three-quarters of which was performed by Mlle Dubuquoy, whose ingenious hint that Marie Antoinette was fond of such employments had inspired Josephine's inclination for them. At the other side of the chimney sat Mlle Hortense Beauharnais, an amiable, mild, agreeable girl with the figure of a nymph and beautiful light hair. Her gracious manners and gentle words were irresistibly pleasing.

The First Consul was standing before the chimney with his hands behind him, fidgeting as he had already the habit of doing; his eyes were fixed upon me. . . .

Mme Bonaparte stood up, came forward, took my two hands and embraced me, saying that I might depend upon her friendship. 'I have been too long Junot's friend', she continued, 'not to entertain the same sentiments for his wife, particularly for the one he has chosen.'"

Rosa Stylosa

he Bonaparte ladies were actively encouraged to support patriotism and home industries. Hortense recalled:

"France prospered, the government became organised and work abounded. Luxury, an indispensable feature of a great state, began to rear its head. In order to revive the cloth industry at Lyon and to set us free from a constant levy we were paying to the British, the First Consul had forbidden us to wear muslin and threw anything he suspected to have been made in England into the fire. Whenever my mother and I appeared before him, all dressed up, his first question was always: 'Is that muslin you're wearing?' Often we replied that it was St-Quentin linen, but a smile invariably betrayed us and instantly his hand would tear the foreign garment asunder. These sartorial disasters recurred frequently, and we had to turn to satin and velvet instead. Fashion intervened, however, and cashmere shawls – in spite of frequent threats to burn them – survived banishment."

Rosa Alpina debilis

Rosa Sempervirens latifolia

Rosa Centifolia Anglica rubra

 fter a time Napoleon and Josephine began to quarrel over his extramarital escapades. This letter is addressed from the First Consul, at Boulogne, to Mme Bonaparte, at St-Cloud, Year XII, 19th Brumaire (11 November 1803), at midnight:

"Josephine, your letter was a sad one. You are wrong to think me indifferent to the things that concern you. Your happiness is bound with mine. The feelings you have aroused in me for so long cannot be altered except by yourself. The good, tender Josephine cannot be erased from my heart by anyone except Josephine herself, who by her own doing has become melancholy, irritable and troublesome. My life is made up of many cares, and only a sweet, loving domestic life that is free from all restrictions can help me to endure them.

The gods have been irksome, and so it seems that it must be my destiny to love you always, for I have finally neglected them. I do not know whether this letter will be to your liking. My intention is to console you, my destiny to please you, and my will to love you."

osephine replied to her husband the following day:

"All my worries vanished after reading your kind and touching letter, with such a courteous expression of your feelings for me. I am so grateful that you can devote so much time to your Josephine. If you knew how very much I am grateful to you for this you would congratulate yourself on being able to bring such intense happiness to the woman who loves you. A letter is the portrait of the soul, and I clasp yours to my heart. It makes me feel so good! I shall keep it. It will console me in your absence, be my guide when I am near you, because I wish always to remain in your eyes that good, tender Josephine whose only concern is for your happiness. If a feeling of joy passes through your soul, if sadness should trouble you for a moment,

Rosa Noisettiana

it shall be on the bosom of your beloved that you will tell of your happiness and your cares. You will nourish no feeling I will not share. All my prayers, all my wishes strive only to please you and to make you happy.... Adieu, Bonaparte, I shall not forget the last sentence of your letter. It is locked in my heart. How deeply it is carved upon it! My heart meets you with so much delight! Yes, my wish is to please you, to love you, nay, to adore you...."

Rosa Parviflora

Rosa Centifolia foliacea

Rosa Nivea

umours that Napoleon wished to place himself in an even higher position were rife. Hortense wrote:

"I was astonished one day when Caroline [the younger of the Bonaparte sisters, married to Murat], visiting me at home, first told me of the rumours that were circulating about the elevation of the Consul to the Empire.

'They say', she went on, 'that only Joseph and Louis are nominated in the *senatus consultum*. So your children shall be princes, then heirs to the throne of France, and mine, their cousins, shall be nothing. I shall never tolerate this injustice. I shall raise them to uphold their rights, and reclaim them.'

I was at a loss to understand Caroline's rage, her husband being merely the Consul's brother-in law, but I could foresee enemies for my children, and this worried me. In order to console her, I expressed my doubts about the rumours, but it was in vain; nothing would calm her down. Her sister Elisa shared her feelings and indeed kindled them. They created such a fuss that their complaints reached the Consul, who one day said:

'To listen to my sisters, would it not be true to say that I have robbed my family of the inheritance of the dead king, our father?'

This comment, repeated throughout Paris, was considered very sharp. Nevertheless the Emperor's sisters were made princesses. . . ."

Rosa Tomentosa

Rosa Gallica granatus

hancellor Cambacérès, President of the Senate, together with members of the Senate, brought the *senatus consultum* to St-Cloud on 18 May 1804, and addressed Josephine with these words:

"Madame, the Senate has a most agreeable task to perform, in begging to pay Your Imperial Majesty its respects, and express to you the gratitude of the French people. Yes, Madame, fame makes public your constant good works. It tells us that there is always a place in your heart for the unfortunate, and you use your influence with the head of state only to lighten their misfortune and that Your Majesty combines the joy of giving with that delightful gentleness which makes gratitude the sweeter and any benefit the more precious. Such a disposition presages that the Empress Josephine's name will become the symbol of consolation and hope; just as the virtues of Napoleon will always serve as an example to his successors, to teach them the art of governing nations, the living memory of your charity shall teach their august spouses that drying people's tears is the surest way to reign over their hearts. The Senate takes the greatest pride in being the first to greet your Imperial Highness, and he who has the honour of being your subject has the boldness to hope that you will deign to count him among your most faithful servants."

almaison, *mala mansio*, evil house – the name does not bode well. Surrounded by pleasant gardens, it is situated on the left bank of the Seine in beautiful countryside which was then beyond the Paris city walls. The derivation of its sinister name is not known. One theory is that this was the place where Viking plunderers disembarked in 826, or, alternatively, that it refers to the evil deeds perpetrated by a Viking leader on the local women. Another theory is that a leper colony once occupied the site. Documents dating from 1390 tell us of the existence of the château, which remained in the hands of the same family until 1766.

Under a subsequent owner, during the time of Louis XVI, Sophie de Couteulx held a *salon* here. It was attended by the painter Elisabeth Vigée-Lebrun, by the Abbé Siéyès, who was to play such an important part in the Revolution and in the seizing of power by General Bonaparte on 18th Brumaire. Another visitor was the Abbé Delille – an abbé because he enjoyed the benefit of the Abbey of St-Séverin, although he had taken no holy orders himself – who had become famous for his translations of Virgil's *Georgics* and became a member of the French Academy at the age of thirty-six. The verses quoted at the beginning of each chapter of this book are taken from his series of descriptive poems, *Les Jardins*.

The roof-tops of Malmaison were visible from the Bauldry house at Croissy, across the Seine, where Citizeness Beauharnais lived after being released from prison under the Terror. General Bonaparte wanted a country property 'near Paris or in Burgundy', as he confided to his brother Joseph. His wife bought the château, land, and furniture for him for 250,000 francs, without actually having the money to pay for it.

From the minor recesses of French history Malmaison was catapulted into notoriety. Josephine, who was very fond of the house, retired there

Opposite above: Malmaison seen from the park, watercolour by Louis Garneray. Opposite below: Malmaison from the stone bridge, watercolour by Louis Garneray.

Right: Malmaison, tapestry decorated with vases of flowers and birds. Below: The Empress's music-room, watercolour by Auguste Garneray.

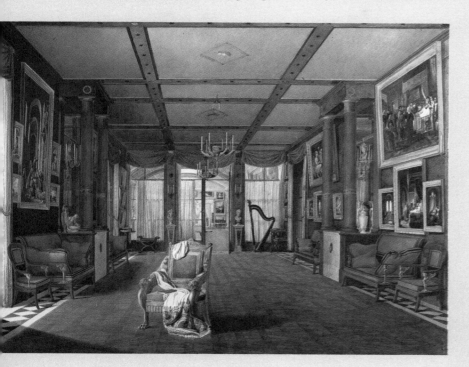

after her divorce from Napoleon and died there. The First Consul used to spend weekends there, or rather 'decade-ends' (the Republican calendar worked in units of ten days), and would hold meetings there with his counsellors, preparing edicts or laws.

When Josephine bought the house, it was in a bad state of repair. Two architects, Fontaine and Percier, worked on restoring Malmaison, though both were later replaced by Lepère. Fontaine noted in his diary that under Napoleon Malmaison underwent continual refurbishment and extension:

"The chance of fame for ourselves, by building on the most beautiful site of Malmaison a dwelling worthy of the great man in whose service we find ourselves, is regretfully slipping away from us. We are asked instead to restore and make comfortable a bad

When Josephine bought Malmaison, the property included a small park and some horticultural land and vineyards. On her death in 1814 there was three times as much parkland, without counting the attached land. The Garneray family, comprising the father, who was a pupil of David's and well known for his portrait of Charlotte Corday, and his three sons, illustrated Malmaison and its park in a series of elegant watercolours. From this series: Right, rhododendron bushes and the little Temple of Love, which a witness maintains was inspired by the Temple of Clitumnus; Below, the greenhouse. Bottom: The black swans of the Bass Strait at Malmaison, from the Collection des Vélins.

house which is falling into ruin, and which had originally been built for a very ordinary person."

A grand hall was added, together with the Council Room, a library, a billiard-room, and a gallery to house all those works of art that were the spoils of the Italian campaign. The interior was redecorated and apartments refurbished. The gardens were embellished with rustic little bridges, statues, columns, summer-houses, a little temple, and a large neo-classical greenhouse. Gradually the property was extended to take on the Butard and Jonchère forests, the Buzenval Park and Château together with the Mélannière woods, the Château de la

Chaussée, and the forest of St-Cucufa, where Josephine had a Swiss chalet built for the Bernese cowherd who tended her Swiss cows.

The pastimes of Malmaison, the schoolboy games, and the amateur dramatics have already been described. Laure Junot recalled:

"No sight could be more exhilarating than a ball at Malmaison, composed of the numerous young women connected with the military household which the First Consul had just formed, and who constituted, without having yet received the name, the court of Mme Bonaparte. All were young, many were pretty ... when

this beautiful group was attired in robes of white crêpe trimmed with flowers, and their hair ornamented with garlands as fresh as the complexion of their merry faces, smiling with happiness and good humour. It was a charming and striking spectacle to see the animated dance which derived its zest from their gaiety, in the same room in which the First Consul and the most renowned characters of Europe were promenading."

Josephine's passion for her flowers grew. Ventenat, in dedicating the *Jardin de la Malmaison* to her, which was written by him and illustrated by Redouté, penned the following words:

"Madame, you have understood that a liking for flowers should not be a sterile study. You have gathered under your eyes some of the rarest plants on French soil. Tended by you, many plants that had never before left the deserts of Arabia and the scorching sands of Egypt have become acclimatized and now, classified in the usual way, they represent in the beautiful garden of Malmaison the sweetest memory of your illustrious husband's conquests, and the most agreeable evidence of your studious leisure."

Là, sont des animaux, étrangères merveilles.
Là, dans un doux exil vivent emprisonnés
Quadrupèdes, oiseaux, l'un de l'autre étonnés . . .
Offrez-nous ces oiseaux qui, nés sous d'autres cieux,
Favoris du soleil, brillent de tous ses feux,
L'or pourpré du faisan, l'émail de la pintade.
Logez plus richement ces oiseaux de parade;
Eux-mêmes sont un luxe, et puisque leur beauté
Rachette à vos regards leur inutilité,
De ces captifs brillans que les prisons soient belles.

Yon latticed fence what exiled people own,
Who strike the astonished sense with sounds unknown?
These curious foreigners, of various kind,
Surprised to meet, an easy durance find . . .
Those feathered natives of more glowing skies,
Those birds, bright favourites of the sun, we prize,
Who own his fires, and boast unnumbered dies.
There let us view the pheasant's purpled gold,
There the pintado's speckled garb behold.
A prison more magnificent prepare,
To hold these brilliant captives of the air,
Themselves a luxury, their want of use
Nature compensates, of their charms profuse.

From Delille, *Les Jardins*, IV

The Empress Josephine

1804–1809

Rosa Hudsoniana Salicifolia

Rosa Gallica agatha incarnata

apoleon's coronation as Emperor took place at Notre Dame, Paris, on 2 December 1804, and Mme de Rémusat was there to record it:

"Before setting out for Notre Dame we were admitted to the apartment of the Empress. Our attire was very brilliant, but it paled before the magnificence of the costumes of the imperial family. The Empress especially, sparkling with diamonds and wearing her hair in countless curls, a style of the time of Louis XVI, did not look more than twenty-five [she was in fact forty-one]. She wore a white satin gown and a court mantle of the same material, both profusely embroidered in mingled gold and silver. Her ornaments consisted of a diadem, a necklace, earrings and a girdle of diamonds of immense value, and all this gorgeous attire was worn with her customary easy grace. Her sisters-in-law were also adorned with a vast quantity of jewels. The Emperor inspected each of us in her turn, smiling at this luxury, which was, like all the rest, a sudden creation of his sovereign will."

Bearing the train of the imperial mantle were Caroline (Bonaparte Murat), Elisa (Bonaparte Bacciocchi), Paulette (Bonaparte Borghese), and Julie Clary (wife of Joseph Bonaparte). The Empress, weighed down by the heavy train, reached a point where it was obvious that she could not proceed.

"When she had to walk from the altar to the throne there was a slight altercation with her sisters-in-law, who carried her mantle with such an ill grace that I observed at one moment the new-made Empress could not advance a step. The Emperor perceived this and spoke a few sharp short words to his sisters, which speedily brought them to reason."

Constant, Napoleon's valet, described Josephine's crown thus:

"It had eight fronds that were joined under a golden sphere, which was surmounted by the cross. The fronds were decorated with diamonds, four in the shape of palm leaves, four in the shape of myrtle leaves. Around it there was a band studded with eight enormous emeralds. The band that rested on her forehead glittered with amethysts. Her diadem was made up of four strings of the finest pearls, interwoven with diamond foliage, perfectly mounted, and set with a skill which was as admirable as the richness of the jewels themselves. On the front of the crown there were several large diamonds, one of which alone weighed 149 grains. The crown was surrounded by a ribbon of gold embellished by 39 pink stones."

The Duchesse d'Abrantès recalls:

"Napoleon took a complacent delight in the sight of the Empress as she advanced towards him, and when she knelt down – when the tears which she could not suppress fell upon her clasped hands, as they were raised to Heaven, or rather to

Rosa Rubiginosa Vaillantiana

Napoleon – both then appeared to enjoy one of those fleeting moments of pure felicity which are unique in a lifetime. . . . The Emperor performed with peculiar grace every action required of him during the ceremony, but his manner of crowning Josephine was most remarkable. After receiving the small crown surmounted by the cross, he had first to place it on his own head, and then to transfer it to that of the Empress. When the moment arrived for placing the crown on the head of the woman whom popular superstition regarded as his good genius, his manner was almost playful. He took great pains to arrange this little crown, which was placed over Josephine's tiara of diamonds. He put it on, then took if off, and finally put it on again, as if to promise her she would wear it gracefully and lightly."

Rosa Eglanteria sub rubra

Rosa Rubifolia

Rosa Biserrata

lle d'Avrillion, the Empress's *femme de chambre*, described how Napoleon and Josephine in some ways resembled the most ordinary couple in the world:

"Sometimes the Emperor would come in during the Empress's toilet, and it was extraordinary for us to see a man whose head was so full of important matters enter into such minute detail and indicate which clothes and jewellery the Empress should wear on this or that occasion. One day he happened to stain a gown with ink because he did not care for it, and in order to force the Empress to wear something else. Whenever he touched her jewel caskets he left everything in disarray. . . ."

He wrote to her from Boulogne, while she was taking the waters at Plombières, in Year XIII, 25th Thermidor (13 August 1805):

"I hardly ever hear of you. It's a pity you forget your friends. I did not know before that Plombières water has the same properties as the river of Lethe.
I can fancy you drinking this Plombières water, and saying: 'Ah, Bonaparte, if I die, who will be left to love you?' But that's a long way off, isn't it? Everything has its end – beauty, wit, feeling, the sun itself: but what will never end is the happiness that I desire, the good fortune that – who is it? – enjoys, and the kindness of my Josephine. If you laugh at me, I shall never make love to you again.
Goodbye, darling. I made an attack on the English cruiser yesterday. All went well."

*Rosa Gallica agatha
(Varietas parva violacea)*

lle d'Avrillion recalled:

"The Emperor would sometimes give us a friendly slap or pull our ears. He did not bestow these favours on everyone, and we could gauge his good humour from the degree to which he hurt us. One day, when he was apparently happier than usual, he pinched my cheek so hard that I screamed. . . . I bore the visible trace of His Majesty's satisfaction on my face for several days. He often did the same with the Empress, while we were dressing her. He would punch her playfully, preferably on her shoulders, and she would say in vain: 'Stop, stop it, Bonaparte,' but he would continue for as long as the game amused him. The Empress forced herself to laugh, but more than once I saw tears in her eyes. She behaved towards him with consistent sweetness, and with a kindness such as I have never seen in anyone.''

Josephine's *femme de chambre* described certain domestic changes that took place after the coronation:

"The coronation wrought more changes in the palace than the very foundation of the empire had done. From that moment everything assumed a different complexion and relations between Their Majesties naturally underwent some considerable changes. The Emperor had continued to spend the night in the Empress's apartments as he had done when he was First Consul. From the coronation onwards, however, he slept in his own apartments and it was only seldom that the couple spent the night together. There was a hidden room whereby the Emperor could go down to the Empress's apartments from his own; since he was an early riser he often went down before his wife got up. At other times, since he liked to retire early, he would have her summoned from his bed, and the Empress would drop everything in order to meet his every wish, which she had grown accustomed to equate with orders. The Emperor was very fond of talking with her, and their conversations would often last for hours on end; she would frequently read books to him; he was very fond of hearing her read aloud. When the Emperor was on the point of yielding to sleep, the Empress would go down the little staircase and find her drawing-room as she had left it, because guests did not break up their party whenever the Emperor sent for the Empress, and on her return the conversation or card game would be resumed at the point where she had had to interrupt them.''

Rosa Centifolia Burgundiaca

Rosa Indica Stelligera

Mlle d'Avrillion tells us about Josephine's obsession with buying and acquiring possessions.

"Josephine was inordinately partial to beautiful things. All *objets d'art*, regardless of their price, had to belong to her, and in any case she did not have the courage to send a tradesman away without buying something from him. She bought extremely expensive objects which she had no use for, purely for the pleasure of buying them. It could not even be said that she had a particular predilection for specific things; all objects of good taste appealed to her equally, and she needed them. No one had such exquisite taste as she; artists, artisans and merchants all strove to offer her their wares, and all of them were accepted.

The bills flooded in and her expenditure always greatly exceeded the allowance allotted to her, much of which went on charity. Invariably she had to turn to the Emperor, who always ended up by paying, but only after scenes so heated that they resulted in violence. The Emperor would fly into a rage, the Empress would weep, and an agreement would put a stop to the scenes. These were so painful for the Empress that she would firmly resolve not to give the Emperor further reason to repeat them, but her natural propensity had the stronger pull, and she would resume her spending. Malmaison certainly cost her a great deal in tears!"

On her flowers (also from Mlle d'Avrillion):

"Aimé Bonpland, keeper of those magnificent gardens [at Malmaison] was a highly distinguished scholar, and a close friend of the celebrated Humboldt. At Malmaison he devoted himself to filling the greenhouses with the rarest plants, and the Empress acquired such a passion for them that her spending rose greatly. I saw her pay 3000 francs for one bulb, the name of which I forget. Her taste for botany was no mere caprice, but the basis of study, and serious study at that. She soon knew the names of all the plants, the family they were classified as belonging to by naturalists, their origins and their properties. She took great pleasure in visiting her greenhouses; her little walks always led her in that direction."

About her animals Mlle d'Avrillion tells us:

"The halls of Malmaison resembled an aviary. All around were cages in large quantities, containing the rarest of birds, of whom Her Majesty was a great lover. . . . One of the Empress's favourite pursuits at Malmaison was to visit the pheasantry, and all the other animals, which had become quite tame. There were many beautiful golden pheasants from China, and the stream was inhabited by a mass of waterbirds of all species. Most unusual of all, however, were two black swans of the most striking beauty, which frequently hatched cygnets; they were the only ones that had been able to survive in France. For a while Her Majesty kept various gazelles, charming and graceful animals that roamed freely, coming and going as they wished in the park at Malmaison."

Rosa Indica Sertulata

Rosa Pimpinellifolia inermis

Rosa Sepium flore submultiplici

Rosa Gallica agatha
(var. regalis)

Rosa Bifera pumila

Rosa arvensis ovata

apoleon was now at a high point in his conquest of Europe. He wrote to the Empress from Austerlitz, just after the battle, on 12th Frimaire, Year XIV (3 December 1805):

"I have sent you Lebrun from the battlefield. I have defeated the Russian and Austrian armies, led by the two Emperors. I had some difficulty in doing so, and was obliged to spend eight days in the open air, with some very chilly nights. Tonight I shall sleep in Prince Kaunitz's castle, where I will rest for two or three hours. The Russian army is not merely defeated, but destroyed. I embrace you. Napoleon."

Two days later he wrote further:

"I have secured a truce. The Russians are retreating. The Battle of Austerlitz is one of the finest I have ever waged. Forty-five flags, more than 150 cannon, the standards of the Russian guard, 20 generals, 30,000 prisoners, more than 20,000 killed – a dreadful sight! The Emperor

Rosa Gallica Stapeliae flora

Alexander is in despair and is leaving for Russia. He has shown neither talent nor bravery. Yesterday at my camp I met the Emperor of Austria. We talked for two hours. We agreed on a forthcoming peace. The weather as yet is not too inclement. The continent has its peace back. We must hope that the world has the same. The English will not be able to cope with us. I am so looking forward to seeing you again. There is an eye infection going around, which I have as yet been spared from. Goodbye, my good friend. I am very well and longing to embrace you. Nap.''

Two days later:

"I have agreed an armistice. Peace will follow in about a week. I would like to know if you reached Munich in good health. The Russians are retreating. Their losses are devastating: more than 20,000 dead and 30,000 taken prisoner. Their army is reduced by three-quarters. Buxhoewden, their general-in-chief, is dead. I have 3000 wounded, and between 700 and 800 dead. My eyes hurt a little: it is a disease which is spreading, but it is nothing. Goodbye, my friend. I so want to see you again. Tonight I shall sleep in Brünn. Nap.''

He arrived in Brünn and wrote to Josephine again on 10 December:

"I have not had news of you for a long time now. Do the parties in Baden, Stuttgart and Munich make you forget the poor soldiers who are covered in mud, rain and blood? I am leaving shortly for Vienna. We are working towards consolidating the peace. The Russians have retreated and are fleeing far away from here, going back to Russia well and truly defeated and very humiliated. I do so wish I could be beside you again. Goodbye, my friend. N. My eye trouble is getting better.''

Two days later he wrote her another letter from Brünn, still pathetically pleading, still admirably patient, though now with a touch of irony.

"Great Empress, not a single letter since your departure from Strasbourg. You have passed through Baden, Stuttgart and Munich without writing a single word to us. That is neither very loving, nor very tender. I am still in Brünn. The Russians have left. I have a truce. In a few days I will know the outcome. Please deign, from the lofty heights of your greatness, to devote a little time to your slaves. N.''

Rosa Gallica agatha
(var prolifera)

 marriage was arranged between Prince Eugène and Princess Augusta of Bavaria. Napoleon sent for Eugène, to meet his bride-to-be in Munich. Mlle d'Avrillion takes up the story:

"The Prince whom the Emperor had sent for so hurriedly had travelled all day and all night. On his arrival the Empress was still in bed; when I went into her room and announced he was in Munich, she cried a good deal at the knowledge that he had not come to see her first. I witnessed this encounter.

The Emperor held Prince Eugène by the hand and, pushing him forward, said: 'There you are, Madam, there is your foolish son. . . .' Her Majesty embraced him in tears. No one could fail to recognize her rebuke to the Emperor for having introduced her son to his bride-to-be without her having seen him beforehand. The Prince had a moustache, but his mother felt he looked better without one.

'Why', she said to the Emperor, 'did you introduce Eugène before he could shave his moustache, and without giving him time to make himself look presentable?' This remark, delivered with all the passion that inevitably follows tears, made the Emperor smile, and he cheerfully apologized for not having thought of such important matters. The Empress feared that her son's appearance might not have contributed to a favourable first impression. She made such a fuss that he finally consented to sacrifice his moustache. . . ."

Eugène married Princess Augusta on 14 January 1806, and it turned out to be a happy marriage. The union between Hortense and Napoleon's brother Louis, however, was quite the reverse.

Rosa Indica dichotoma

Rosa Collina Monsoniana

On 7 January 1807 the Emperor wrote to the Empress from Warsaw, where he met Marie Walewska, his future mistress. Clearly Josephine had expressed a wish to follow his winter campaigns more closely than he thought suitable, and he was worried about her comfort and safety.

"My friend, I am deeply moved by what you tell me, but the weather is cold, the roads bad and unsafe, and I cannot therefore allow you to expose yourself to so much discomfort and danger. Go to the Tuileries, receive people and lead the same life you are accustomed to leading when I am there. That is my wish. It may be that I will not be long in joining you, but it is essential that you give up your notion of travelling 300 leagues in this season, through hostile countries and at the rear of the army. Believe me, it hurts me more than it hurts you to have to delay the joy of seeing you again by a few weeks, but necessity and circumstances dictate it. Goodbye, my good friend. Be happy and remember to display the character and behaviour of an Empress. N."

On the seventeenth he wrote to her from Osterode:

"My friend, you really must not attend cheap performances and sit in any old box – it does not become your position. You must only go to the four main theatres, and always sit in the imperial box. Lead the life you led when I was in Paris. My health is excellent. The weather has turned cold: the thermometer fell to 8 degrees. All yours, Nap."

Two days later he wrote again, less facetiously:

"I hate having to be away from you; the harshness of this climate weighs heavily on my soul. Everyone misses Paris here, Paris for whose sake we incessantly chase after glory. And all this, basically, Josephine, in order to be applauded on our return from the stalls at the Opéra. When spring comes, I hope to teach the Russians a lesson, and afterwards, ladies, we shall make our way to you, and you shall give us our laurels. Napoleon."

Rosa farinosa

Rosa Indica Caryophyllea

the valet who accompanied her that she had been banished for having put on too many airs."

Rosa Gallica Pontiana

Hortense described her mother's fears at this time.

"All the soldiers set off for Spain. Caroline left for Naples. My mother and I accompanied the Emperor to Rambouillet, whence he left to join the army in Spain [30 October 1808]. The Empress was even sadder than usual to see the Emperor go.

'Will you never cease your warmongering?' she asked him.

I remember that the Emperor replied, 'Do you think I do it for sport? Don't you think I would prefer to stay peacefully in my comfortable bed

May 1808 saw the Congress of Bayonne, at which Napoleon forced the abdication of the two Bourbon Kings of Spain, father and son, Charles IV and Ferdinand VII, unleashing a host of troubles.

Victor, Duc de Broglie, observed that Josephine's charms were waning:

"I saw the Empress walk by with great pomp, followed by a splendid retinue of ladies of honour that constituted our sultan's harem and helped him patiently to endure the whitewashed old age of his distinguished consort a little longer. It seems, however, that the bargain struck between the imperial couple was not without its conditions. A few days later we saw one of those odalisques file past in tears, and we learned from

Rosa muscosa

Rosa Damascena Celsiana prolifera

Rosa Bifera macrocarpa

and eat good meals, rather than endure all the deprivations that lie ahead of me? Do you think I am any different from anyone else? Come now, of course I could do other things than go to war, but I am bound by necessity, by my duty to France, and I cannot dispose of events: I merely obey them.'

The war began under such sad auspices that everyone felt vaguely uneasy about it. There was no trace of that usual warring enthusiasm I had witnessed so often before. . . ."

By now Josephine lived in fear of a divorce, of which too many people had already spoken. Just over a year later her worst fears were realized.

Captain Coignet's *Cahiers* tell us about the detailed rumours that were circulating among the army:

"The Emperor may have been pleased with us, but we were certainly not pleased with him. Rumours were circulating among the guards that he was divorcing his wife in order to take an Austrian princess in payment for the expenses of the second war with the Emperor of Austria, and that he wanted an heir to the throne. To achieve this, he had to banish the *femme accomplie* and take as his bride a stranger who was to restore an overall peace."

Rosa Venteriatiana

Rosa Reclinata flore simplici

On 30 November 1809 the divorce was announced. Bausset, the prefect of the palace, refers to the incident:

"Their Majesties sat at table, Josephine wearing a wide-brimmed white hat, tied under her chin, which concealed part of her face. I fancied she had been crying, and was forcing herself not to start again. Utter silence reigned throughout dinner, the couple merely picking at their food for the sake of appearances. The only words spoken were by Napoleon, who asked me, 'What is the weather like?' In saying this, he rose from the table. Josephine followed him slowly. Coffee was served, and Napoleon took his cup, proffered by the page, and gestured that he wanted to be left alone.

I sat down in the hall outside, on a chair near the door that led into the Emperor's drawing-room. As I looked on mechanically as the servants cleared the table, I suddenly heard Josephine scream violently from the Emperor's drawing-room. The usher made to open the door. I stopped him, remarking that the Emperor would call for help as and when he thought it necessary.

I was standing next to the door when Napoleon opened it and said: 'Come in, Bausset, and close the door behind you.' I went into the drawing-room and found the Empress lying on the carpet, screaming and weeping piteously.

'I shall not survive this,' the unfortunate woman kept saying.

Napoleon asked me: 'Are you strong enough to lift Josephine, carry her down the inner staircase to her bedroom, and minister to her as necessary?'

I obeyed, and helped the Empress – whom I judged to be suffering from an attack of nerves – to her feet. With Napoleon's help I lifted her up. He took a candlestick from the table, lit the way for me, and opened the door to a dark passageway that led to the inner staircase he had mentioned. Having gone down the first step, I realized that the area was too narrow to go on without risk of falling.

The Emperor at once called the servant who guarded the door of his study day and night, for the room overlooked the landing of the little inner staircase. Napoleon handed him the candlestick, which he had little need of, since those passageways were already lit. He ordered the servant to proceed, himself taking Josephine's legs in order to help me down.

When I had helped her up, in the drawing-room, the Empress had calmed down and I thought she must be ill, but when I tripped over my sword halfway down the staircase I was obliged to tighten my grip on her, to avoid a fall that would have brought all the protagonists of the unfortunate scene to the floor. I held the Empress with my arms round her waist, her back against my chest and her head resting on my right shoulder. When she became aware of the effort I was making to avoid falling, she whispered to me: 'You are holding me too tightly.' I then realized there was no reason to fear for her health, and that she had in fact been conscious throughout the proceedings. . . .

Napoleon, in his distress, revealed to me what had happened.

'The interests of France and the dynasty have ravaged my heart. . . . Divorce has become a harsh duty for me . . . the scene Josephine made therefore distresses me all the more. . . . Three days ago Hortense had to tell her of the unhappy obligation that condemns me to be separated from her. . . . I pity her with all my heart. I thought her character would have enabled her to withstand the blow, and I was not prepared for such a painful outburst.'

Because he was so upset he had to make long pauses between sentences in order to draw breath. The disjointed words tumbled out of him painfully. His saddened voice quivered, and his eyes were wet with tears. . . .''

Rosa Gallica Maheka
(flore subsimplici)

Rosa Hispida argentea

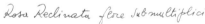
Rosa Reclinata flore submultiplici

Rosa sepium myrtifolia

osephine's last public appearance as Empress was at a reception given by the prefect of the Seine, Count Frochot, at the Hôtel de Ville on 4 December 1809. The Duchess d'Abrantès described the scene:

"We went up to the throne room, and had scarcely taken our seats before the drums announced the Empress's arrival. Never shall I forget her appearance on that day, or the costume which so admirably became her. Her countenance, always gentle, was on that occasion veiled in grief. . . . When she approached that throne upon which she was about to sit in the presence of the great city, perhaps for the last time, her legs failed her, her eyes filled with tears, and she had to sit down quickly. She must have felt ready to collapse, yet her face was wreathed

in smiles! Oh, the tortures of a crown! I sought her eyes the moment she sat down, and would willingly have fallen at her feet to tell her how much I felt for her. She understood, and cast upon me a look of the deepest melancholy which, perhaps, her eyes had never expressed since that crown, now robbed of its roses, had been placed upon her head."

lle d'Avrillion wrote of that occasion:

"That day the Empress made her toilet as usual. Yet in spite of her efforts to conceal the pain she felt, one would have had to be blind not to see, from the redness round her eyes, how much she had wept. Her sad and defeated air was painful to behold, but her stable mood did not falter for a moment. I noticed that she kept casting her eye

Rosa l'Heritieranea

Rosa Alba Cimbrefolia

on a sheet of paper, and I could see that it was the speech she would have to make before the Emperor, and it had been given to her so she could learn it off by heart.''

Hortense described the formalities:

"Finally, on 15 December 1809, the day of the divorce, the entire family gathered in the Emperor's study where he was alone with the Empress. Everyone took their seats according to their rank. The arch-chancellor and Count Regnaud de St-Jean-d'Angély entered the room and remained standing. The Emperor produced a document which he read aloud in a strong voice, but when he came to the words: 'She has adorned my life for fifteen years,' his emotion was visible. Then it was the Empress's turn to read. Tears prevented her from continuing. She

handed her document to Count Regnaud who finished reading for her, he too in tears. The statement having been checked and signed by everyone, the Emperor embraced the Empress, took her by the hand and led her into his apartments. A few moments later she came to fetch me. I found her depressed, and prostrate with the self-control she had wilfully imposed on herself. I felt her courage must be sustained right to the end. I reminded her of the unfortunate Queen who had preceded her in this very palace, and who had left it to go to the scaffold. . . .''

Josephine had many friends at all levels of society, and this 'political' divorce was unpopular in Napoleon's armies. During the retreat from Russia in 1812 Major Paquin, an old soldier, was heard to say: 'There was no call for him to leave the "old girl". She brought him luck, and us too.'

'I am happy to see these foreign plants flourish and multiply,' wrote Josephine to Thibaudeau on 28th Ventôse of Year XII (19th March 1804).

"I wish Malmaison soon to offer a model of good cultivation, and to become a source of riches for the rest of France. It is with this in mind that I am having a very large quantity of trees and shrubs from southern countries and South America cultivated. I want each *département* within ten years to possess a collection of rare plants that have originated from my nurseries...."

Thus she built up the public's interest in her passion for gardening. To indulge it, the boycott on trade with England was waived, so that prized plant species could be brought over from the enemy country.

Roses – Rose, after all, was one of Josephine's names – were at the heart of this love for botany, possibly because she felt nostalgia for her childhood on the luxuriant tropical island of Martinique.

The genus *Rosa* covers, depending on the botanist, 70 to 350 spontaneous species originating in the Northern Hemisphere, and particularly in the mountain regions of the tropics. Wild roses are not found in the Southern Hemisphere. Twenty-five thousand garden roses derived from these have been described, most of which enjoyed only a brief lifespan. According to a note by Edmond Launert to one of the editions of Pierre-Joseph Redouté's rose books, only a limited number of wild rose bushes are involved in the cultivation of roses in France up to the nineteenth century. Quoted in this note are the damask rose (*Rosa damascena*), the white rose (*Rosa × alba*), a natural hybrid already cultivated by the Romans, and the *Rosa centifolia*, or Provençal rose, the wild variety of which is found in the Caucasus, and from which Dutch gardeners of the seventeenth century and later obtained several different varieties. The three rose bushes mentioned above, whose perfume is reputed to be a great

Roses de Provins Simples

Roses de Provins doubles

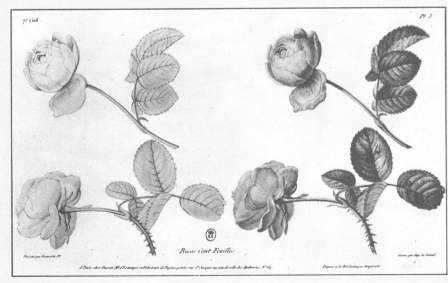

Roses Cent Feuilles

aphrodisiac, played an important role in the perfume trade, particularly in eighteenth-century France, and were widely cultivated for this purpose. Modern methods require at least 700kg (1544lb) of petals to obtain 1kg (about $2\frac{1}{4}$lb) of rose essence, and in the past the necessary quantity of petals would have been much greater.

An older rose to be found in European gardens is the rose of Jericho, or *Rosa gallica*, which was presumably brought from the East in about 1140 by the explorer, Thibaut IV, Count of Champagne and King of Navarre. The origin of the common (Provins rose) name is commercial, deriving from Provins, a city roughly 80km (50 miles) south-east of Paris, which was the main market for these rose bushes. At the beginning of the nineteenth century two further roses appeared in Europe, the China rose and the Bourbon rose. The former, also known as the Bengal rose, bears the Latin name *Rosa chinensis* and was mentioned as far back as 1733. In 1759 it bloomed in London's famous Chelsea Physic Garden, and ten years later also in Princess Augusta's botanic gardens at Kew. New importations guaranteed its importance in gardening during the century that followed. The Bourbon rose was discovered by a keeper of the botanic gardens on Bourbon Island (now known as Réunion), who sent it over to Paris in 1819 to be scrutinized by Louis XVIII. A descendant variety is called *Souvenir de la Malmaison* (memory of Malmaison), a fragrant reminder of those places described by Prince Clary: 'Forests with tall trees, well laid-out lawns, magnificent waters, the long canal where beautiful boats float, and black, purple-necked swans swim.'

Mem. de l'Acad. 1707. Pl. 10. p. 490.

Opposite above: Single Provins rose and double Provins rose, from Tardieu, Le livre des fleurs du XVIIIe siècle. *Opposite below: Rosa centifolia, from Prévost,* Cahier des fleurs et des fruits, *1808. Above: Anatomy of a rose. French engraving, 1707.*

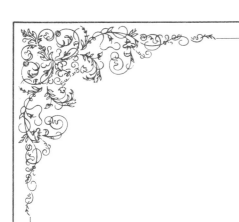

*escends, aimable paix, si long-temps attendue,*
Descends ; que ta présence à l'univers rendue,
Embellisse les lieux qu'ont célébrés mes vers ;
Viens ; forme un peuple heureux de cent peuples divers.
Rends l'abondance aux champs, rends le commerce aux ondes,
Et la vie aux beaux arts, et le calme aux deux mondes.

Descend from Heaven, oh long expected Peace!
Bid sorrow, poverty, and carnage cease,
Smile on the world, on Nature smile, and long
Adorn the landscape, and reward my song;
All nations in one friendly link combine,
And bid the Arts again, bid Genius shine,
Plenty and Commerce to the world restore,
And spread tranquillity from shore to shore.

From Delille, *Les Jardins*, IV

Exile

1809–1814

Rose Centifolia prolifera foliacea

Amid all the rancour of the divorce arose the question of Josephine's hairdresser, as explained by Mlle d'Avrillion:

"For over twenty years Duplan had dressed the Empress's hair. He was a good man, sincerely devoted to Her Majesty, who was herself very attached to him. She was convinced that no one else in the world could do her hair as well as he did, and indeed Duplan continued to cut the Emperor's hair, and was thus the imperial hairdresser. After coming to the throne, the Empress paid him an annuity of 12,000 francs which he retained after he retired to Malmaison.

When Napoleon married the Archduchess Marie-Louise, he decided that no one other than Duplan was fit to dress the new Empress's hair. Duplan was therefore brought before the Emperor, who asked him how much the Empress Josephine paid him.

'Sire,' Duplan replied, 'Twelve thousand francs.'

'I herewith nominate you hairdresser to the Empress Marie-Louise. You may have the money [the 12,000 francs], but I do not wish you to dress anyone else's hair.'

'Sire, the Empress Josephine allowed me to dress other people's hair, and my professional standing enabled me to earn the same fee again from my other clients.'

'So be it! You may have the 24,000 francs, but on condition you dress her hair only, and no one else's.'

Unable to argue further, Duplan consented. When the time came for Josephine's toilet, one of Duplan's pupils arrived instead, bearing a letter of apology from Duplan, in which the hairdresser

Rosa Hudsoniana subcorymbosa

Rosa Rorenbergiana

Rosa Centifolia anemonoïdes

time helped to heal the emotional scars a little. Josephine wrote to her daughter Hortense on 14 June 1810:

"Yesterday was a happy day. The Emperor came to see me. His presence brought me great joy, though it opened my wounds. One would wish to feel such emotions often. During all the time he stayed with me, I had enough courage to keep back the tears I knew were ready to flow, but after he had left I could contain myself no longer and felt very unhappy. He was good, and kind towards me, as always. I hope he could read in my heart all the tenderness and devotion it is imbued with."

expressed his regret at not being able to obey her orders.... The Empress sent for me to tell me what had happened. Two large tears had appeared in her eyes, and her face had changed, clearly not only as a result of what had happened, but because the incident brought back painful memories of the divorce. They were taking away from her a man who had been in her service even before her destiny had been joined with General Bonaparte's, in order to give him to the woman who had taken her place in the imperial bed...."

Rosa Hudsoniana scandens

Rosa alba foliacea

Rosa Gallica Aurelianensis

 he travelled, and lived at Navarre, but her main love was Malmaison. Her friend Mme Georgette Ducrest described how she turned part of it into a shrine for the man she still loved:

"The Empress, still nourishing an attachment for the Emperor that bordered on a cult, had forbidden any furniture in his apartments to be moved from its original position; and instead of occupying his apartments, she preferred to live less comfortably on the first floor. Everything in the Emperor's study was exactly as he had left it. A history book lay on the desk, with a bookmark in the place where he had interrupted his reading. The pen he had used was filled with ink, and seemed as though it might dictate the laws of Europe at any minute. A globe, on which he showed those in whom he could confide the future projects he had in mind and the countries he wanted to conquer, bore the signs of a sudden impatient movement which may have been brought about by a mild disagreement. Josephine alone had taken charge of dusting what she called her relics, and would only rarely allow anyone into this sanctuary. Napoleon's Roman bed had no drapes, there were weapons hanging on the walls, a few items of male clothing were scattered on the furniture. It looked as though he might at any minute enter that room, from which he had banished himself for ever. . . ."

 ow a grandmother, something that consoled her greatly, Josephine wrote from Malmaison to Hortense, who was taking the waters at Aix in Savoy, on 6 August 1813:

Rosa Evratina

Rosa Gallica
(Purpuro-violacea magna)

"The month of August has finally brought us fine, sunny days. I hope they will last, my dear daughter. Your chest will benefit greatly, and the good effects of the waters will be enhanced. I was pleased to notice that you have not forgotten the years of your childhood, and it shows great kindness towards your mother that you should remember them. I was right in making two such good and sensitive children so happy; they have amply recompensed me for this.

Your children shall do the same for you, dear Hortense. Their heart is like yours, they will never cease to love you. Their health is excellent, they have never been fresher or healthier. Little Oui-Oui [the future Napoleon III] is always gallant and charming towards me. Two days ago, witnessing the departure of Mme de Tascher who was leaving to join her husband and take the waters, he said to Mme de Boucheporn: 'She must love her husband very much to leave Grandmamma behind.' Do you not find that enchanting? The same day he went for a walk through the Butard forest and, arriving in the great avenue, he threw his hat up in the air and exclaimed: 'Oh, how I love the beauty of nature!' Few are the days when one or other of them fails to amuse me. They breathe life into everything around me. You can see for yourself how happy you have made me by leaving them with me. I could not be happier, except on the day when you yourself arrive. Goodbye, my dear daughter. I love and embrace you tenderly."

The year before the abortive and appalling Russian campaign had taken place. That autumn, on 16–19 October, Napoleon was to fight the disastrous Battle of Leipzig.

Rosa sempervirens Leschenaultiana

Rosa Gallica guerimiana

After Napoleon's defeat at Leipzig France had been invaded by the Allies. Mme Georgette Ducrest wrote:

"If the sound of the Allied troops advancing had permeated Malmaison, it resounded with no less impact within the walls of the Castle of Navarre, where everyone was shaken by the disasters Napoleon had encountered. Josephine, however, had not abandoned all hope. She was counting on the bravery and skill of the Duke of Ragusa [Marmont], who had been entrusted with the defence of Paris. Her Majesty's position grew more precarious by the minute; she was unaware of what she could hope for or fear. Those who had followed her could finally no longer conceal from her that the capital had surrendered, that the three foreign monarchs had entered the city and that Napoleon had retired to Fontainebleau.

Hearing of the terrible news that had sealed the Emperor's fate, Josephine felt ill and a forlorn silence reigned around her. All the ladies, pale and distressed, seemed to have succumbed to defeat and sorrow.

Gradually becoming herself again and gathering her strength, Josephine exclaimed: 'It is not here that I should stay; it is at the Emperor's side that my presence is needed. I must fulfil what was my duty more than it was Marie-Louise's. The Emperor is alone, forsaken . . . but he still has me left. I could only be separated from him while he was happy. Now I am sure he will be expecting me.'

Tears rolled down her cheeks and her whole being was overtaken by so many memories and bitter sorrows."

On 14 April Josephine, who had hastily sought refuge in Navarre, returned to Malmaison.

Rosa Canina grandiflora

Rosa Indica autumnalis

Napoleon, about to be exiled on Elba, wrote to Josephine from Fontainebleau on 16 April 1814:

"I wrote to you on the eighth of this month (a Friday) and you may not have received my letter. There was still fighting, and it may have been intercepted. Communications have now been restored, however. I have taken my decision. I have no doubt this letter will reach you. I will not repeat the contents of the first letter. In it I complained of my situation, but now I rejoice in it: my head and my soul have been relieved of an enormous burden. My fall is great, but at least, from what they say, it is useful.

In my retirement I shall exchange the sword for the pen. The story of my reign shall be a curious one. It has only ever been shown in profile, and I shall give a complete portrait of myself. There are so many men of whom people have the wrong opinion! . . . I have done many good things for thousands of unfortunate people! What did they, ultimately, do for me? They have betrayed me, yes, one and all, except for the good Eugène, who is so worthy of you and me. May he be happy under a king made for appreciating the sentiments of nature and honour!

Farewell, my dear Josephine. Resign yourself, as I shall, and always remember he who will never forget you. Napoleon.

PS: I shall await your news on the island of Elba. I am not well."

This is believed to be the last letter written to Josephine by Napoleon, who had abdicated ten days earlier.

Rose Bifera Variegata

Mlle d'Avrillion described the visit of Alexander I to Josephine:

"When the Emperor of Russia, Tsar Alexander, discovered that the Empress Josephine had arrived at Malmaison, he hurried to pay his respects. He was kindness itself towards her. When he referred to the occupation of Paris by the Allied troops and Napoleon's position in conversation, he did so guardedly. He never forgot for an instant that he was addressing the former wife of his vanquished enemy. For her part, Josephine never concealed from the Tsar the tender feelings of affection she still felt for the Emperor Napoleon.

Alexander, quite apart from the civilities that sovereigns, like ordinary men, must observe in their dealings with women, was undoubtedly gifted with an elevated, magnanimous character, which forbade him from pronouncing a single word against the misfortune that had befallen his adversaries. For herself, the Empress had only one request to make of him, and that concerned the fate of her children.

Her Majesty was kind enough to tell me of the nature of her conversations with Emperor Alexander, whose visit was promptly followed by visits from other Allied princes. She told me many times that what had irritated Emperor Alexander most was the fact that Napoleon, when talking about him, had designated him the 'Barbarian of the North'. He was deeply hurt by this appellation, and, even having witnessed the hateful foreign presence in the heart of France, one could not have agreed – without being extremely unfair – that Napoleon's expression was suited to the object of his insult. At the time of that first invasion, Emperor Alexander's behaviour was consistently impeccable."

Rosa Noisettiana purpurea

Among the other foreign princes who called on Josephine one was conspicuously absent: the Emperor of Austria, Francis II, Napoleon's father-in-law. It seems he conveyed his excuses via the Prince of Coburg, saying he feared that his visit might displease Josephine. She is said to have retorted pungently: 'Why ever should it? It is not me he dethroned, but his own daughter!'

Still on the subject of princely visits at Malmaison during the last months of Josephine's life, Baron Ménéval observed that frequently three young future emperors were gathered together at Malmaison. They were, in order of seniority, the Archduke Nicholas, future Tsar Nicholas I of Russia, Prince William of Prussia, who would one day be proclaimed Emperor William I of Germany at Versailles after the defeat of France in 1870, and Josephine's grandson, the future Napoleon III, who would wage war against the other two.

Rosa Indica subalba

Rosa Gallica flore giganteo

Rosa Indica fragrans flore simplici

Rosa Pomponia Burgundiaca

osephine's health had now deteriorated badly, and the end was not far away. Hortense described her dying moments:

"The following day, 29 May [1814], which was Pentecost, my brother, who had got out of bed in spite of a fever, came with me early in the morning to visit my mother. At the sight of us she stretched her arms out towards us excitedly, and pronounced some unintelligible words. A few hours later I found her so changed that the terrifying certainty of losing her assailed my spirit for the first time. I was no longer mistress of my despair. I was dragged into the adjacent room.

My brother informed me that they were about to give her the last sacrament, but that the doctors had nevertheless not given up hope altogether. We went to mass to pray for the life that was so precious to us. We were all in tears and everyone around us shared in our sorrow. I went back up again, making a supreme effort to pull myself together in order to tell her calmly of the sacrament she was about to receive, to stem any possible surge of emotion in myself at the imminence of that moment, and to display some confidence that I could pass on to her. After all, I too nourished some hope. But when, entering her room, I noticed the fine changes that had taken place in her features in less than half an hour, I could not find the strength to utter a single word, and without even being able to grasp the hand she stretched out towards me, I fell by the side of the bed. I was taken to my room. I do not know what happened next.

A few moments later my brother hurried in and rushed into my arms, bursting into tears. 'It's all over,' he exclaimed. She had received the last

Rosa Pomponiana muscosa

Rosa Canina Burboniana

sacrament with the greatest resignation and her last breath had, without doubt, been for her unhappy children."

Napoleon, exiled on the island of Elba, learned of Josephine's death from a newspaper sent to him from Genoa by a valet who was returning to France. Louis XVIII, the new King of France, read the following item in the daily police bulletin submitted to him by the Comte de Beugnot:

"The death of Mme de Beauharnais is the source of much regret. This woman was born with kindness and elegance of manner and spirit. . . . Excessively unhappy during her husband's reign, she had taken refuge, against his brutality and his

disdain, in the study of botany. . . . The public was aware of the battles she waged to snatch victims away from Bonaparte and was grateful to her for having begged him to spare the Duc d'Enghien. . . ."

Pierre-Joseph Redouté
The 'Raphael of Flowers'

The 'Raphael of flowers' is the complimentary epithet given by his contemporaries to Pierre-Joseph Redouté, the painter of Josephine's roses. He began to paint at the age of five, and lived to be eighty. He gave painting lessons to Marie Antoinette – who is said to have had so little artistic flair that she quickened her step every time she had to cross the galleries of the Louvre – and his last work was destined for the family of King Louis-Philippe. *Ancien régime*, Revolution, Empire, restoration of the monarchy, Pierre-Joseph Redouté passed through all of them unscathed, painting beautiful flowers and earning money from all the potentates he served under. He nevertheless died in financial straits.

Four years older than Josephine, he was born on 10 July 1759, the fifth of six children, at St-Hubert in Belgium. Painting ran in the family: his father eked out a living from his paintbrush by working for the Ardennes nobility, convents and wealthy members of the bourgeoisie who were anxious to have themselves painted. A brother in Paris worked in the theatre as a props artist, painting scenery for the Commedia dell'Arte. Pierre-Joseph went to stay with this brother, helping him to colour in backcloths and wings, and devoting his spare time to studying and painting plants at the Jardin du Roi. During a journey to Holland he had been fascinated by the flower paintings of Van Huysum and this may have determined his vocation.

His first patron was L'Héritier, a wealthy magistrate with many cultural interests, an amateur botanist, who was the victim of a mysterious assassination in 1800. He persuaded Redouté to devote himself exclusively to botanical illustrations, and provided him with an opportunity to do so. Redouté painted at the Jardin du Roi and in many private gardens, and he met botanists and floriculturists. He followed L'Héritier to London and worked at Kew Gardens. In London he also made the acquaintance of the Italian engraver Francesco Bartolozzi, a useful meeting since it enabled him to acquire the essential technical knowledge of the tools of his craft. On his return to Paris in December 1787 Redouté made the acquaintance of another crucial figure, Gerard van Spaendonck, professor of botanical painting at the Jardin du Roi. Spaendonck was responsible for what is still well known as the Collection des Vélins, a precious collection of natural history illustrations on vellum begun as far back as the seventeenth century which today comprises 6500 items (the black swans of Malmaison, reproduced on page 80 of the present volume, are part of this collection), and he asked Redouté to work on this. In 1788 Marie Antoinette nominated him Dessinateur du Cabinet de la Reine. In order to add to the Queen's artistic education, he would take bunches of flowers from the royal greenhouses, and arrange them in splendid china vases before capturing their transient beauty in delicate watercolours.

His royal pupil was guillotined in 1793; that same year the Belgian artist exhibited his flower paintings at the Salon. An artist at the Academy of Sciences in 1792, and then at the class of Physics and Mathematics when the academies were amalgamated into the Institut de France, then a plant illustrator in the service of the museum when the Collection des Vélins was transferred to the National Museum of Natural History, Pierre-Joseph Redouté continued to paint flowers. His output was impressive: hundreds of plates for the Collection des Vélins; plates for the *Plantarum succulentarum Historia* by the Swiss botanist Augustin-Pyramus de Candolle; and plates for *Figures de la flore des Pyrenées* by Lapeyrouse.

Redouté figured in the list of *savants* who followed General Bonaparte on the expedition to Egypt. He then met Josephine, and undertook the grandiose project of illustrating and describing the flower species in the garden of Malmaison. The *Jardin de la Malmaison* was published periodically in batches of six plates as the work of the botanist Etienne-Pierre Ventenat and the painter Pierre-Joseph Redouté. Twenty issues were published, with 120 illustrations. Those historians who have gone through Josephine's accounts with a toothcomb have declared that from Year XII (1803–4) to 1808 these two men cost her 42,862 and 85,923 francs respectively. Dating from more or less the same period are the eight volumes with 502 plates of the *Liliacées* (1802–16). Napoleon purchased eighty copies as gifts for guests. *Les Roses* was the last work that Josephine, now no longer Empress, commissioned. She was never to see them. The 169 roses reproduced in the present book were published in a folio edition of just five copies between 1817 and 1824. Redouté continued painting flowers and reaping glory: in 1825 he was awarded the Légion d'Honneur.

Between 1827 and 1833 he published a further *Selection of the most beautiful flowers in the vegetable kingdom, a few branches of the most exquisite fruit, sometimes grouped together and frequently animated by insects and butterflies*. Two years later it was the turn of a *Collection of charming flowers chosen from the most attractive in Europe and other parts of the world*. In 1836 he brought out the *Selection of Sixty Roses dedicated to the Queen of the Belgians*. Other roses were to be published posthumously under the title *Bouquet Royal*. A few weeks before his eighty-first birthday the artist was the victim of an apoplectic fit while he was studying a white lily, and he died on 16 June 1840.

The names of the roses of Malmaison are given in Latin and in French, as they appear in the work of Pierre-Joseph Redouté. The numbers refer to the pages of the present volume where the roses are illustrated.

1   *Rosa Damascena*, Rosier de Cels

4   *Rosa Damascena Italica*, La Quatre-Saisons d'Italie

7   *Rosa centifolia*, Rosier à cent feuilles

8   left *Rosa moschata*, Rosier musqué; right *Rosa Gallica latifolia*, Rosier de Provins à grandes feuilles

9   left *Rosa Rubrifolia*, Rosier à feuilles rougeâtres; right *Rosa centifolia Bullata*, Rosier à Feuilles de Laitue

10   *Rosa Berberifolia*, Rosier à feuilles d'Epine-vinette

11   above left *Rosa Lucida*, Rosier Luisant; right *Rosa Bracteata*, Rosier de Macartney; below *Rosa Eglanteria var. punicea*, Rosier Eglantier var. couleur ponceau

12   above *Rosa Pomponia*, Rosier Pompon; below *Rosa Montezuma*, Rosier de Montezuma

13   above *Rosa Indica acuminata*, Rosier des Indes à petales pointus; below *Rosa Indica*, Rosier des Indes

14   below *Rosa Alpina Laevis*, Rosier des Alpes à pedoncule et calice glabres; above *Rosa muscosa multiplex*, Rosier mousseux à fleurs doubles

15   left *Rosa Indica vulgaris*, Rosier des Indes commun; right *Rosa Centifolia mutabilis*, Rosier unique

19   *Rosa Sulfurea*, Rosier jaune de soufre

20   below *Rosa Kamtschatica*, Rosier du Kamtschatka; above *Rosa Villosa, Pomifera*, Rosier Velu Pomifère

21   left *Rosa Clynophylla*, Rosier à feuilles penchées; right *Rosa Gallica officinalis*, Rosier de Provins ordinaire

22   left *Rosa Damascena subalba*, Rosier de Damas à Pétale teinté de rose; right *Rosa Muscosa Anemone-flora*, La Mousseuse de la Flèche

23   left *Rosa Eglanteria*, Rosier Eglantier; right *Rosa Indica fragrans*, Rosier des Indes odorant

24   above *Rosa Centifolia carnea*, Rosier Vilmorin; below *Rosa Centifolia simplex*, Rosier Centfeuilles à fleurs simples

25   above *Rosa Pimpinellifolia Mariaeburgensis*, Rosier de Marienbourg; below *Rosa Carolina Corymbosa*, Rosier de Caroline en Corymbe

26   *Rosa Rubiginosa triflora*, Rosier Rouillé à trois fleurs

27   above left *Rosa Redutea rubescens*, Rosier Redouté à tiges et à épines rouges; right *Rosa Muscosa alba*, Rosier Mousseux à fleurs blanches, below *Rosa Pimpinellifolia Pumila*, Petit Rosier Pimprenelle

31   *Rosa Gallica Versicolor*, Rosier de France à fleurs panachées

32   left *Rosa Brevistyla Leucochroa*, Rosier à court-style (var. à fleurs jaunes et blanches); above right *Rosa Damascena Coccinea*, Rosier de Portland; below *Rosa alba Regalis*, Rosier blanc Royal

33   *Rosa Redutea glauca*, Rosier Redouté à feuilles glauques

34 above *Rosa foetida*, Rosier à fruit fétide; below *Rosa Cinnamomea flore simplici*, Rosier de Mai à fleurs simples

35 above *Rosa Collina fastigiata*, Rosier Nivellé; below *Rosa Indica Pumila*, Rosier main du Bengale

36 above *Rosa Alpina pendulina*, Rosier des Alpes à fruits pendants; below *Rosa bifera officinalis*, Rosier des Parfumeurs

37 left *Rosa Moschata flore semi-pleno*, Rosier Muscade à fleurs semidoubles; right *Rosa Cinnamomea Maialis*, Rosier de Mai

38 *Rosa Andegavensis*, Rosier d'Anjou

39 above *Rosa Rubiginosa Cretica*, Rosier de Crète; below left *Rosa Damascena Variegata*, Rosier d'York et de Lancastre; right *Rosa Rubiginosa Zabeth*, Eglantine de la Reine Elisabeth

43 *Rosa Indica Cruenta*, Rosier du Bengale à fleurs pourpre-de-sang

44 above *Rosa Orbessanea*, Rosier d'Orbessan; below *Rosa Rubiginosa memoralis*, L'Eglantine des bois

45 above *Rosa Gallica Purpurea Velutina, Parva*, Rosier de Van-Eeden; below *Rosa Semper-Virens globosa*, Rosier grimpant à fruits globuleux

46 left *Rosa Gallica rosea flore simplici*, Rosier de Provins à fleurs roses et simples; right *Rosa alba flore pleno*, Rosier blanc ordinaire

47 left *Rosa Centifolia Caryophyllea*, Rosier Oeillet; right *Rosa Turbinata*, Rosier de Francfort

48 above *Rosa Indica subviolacea*, Rosier des Indes à fleurs presque violettes; left *Rosa sepium rosea*, Rosier des hayes à fleurs roses; right below *Rosa Indica Pumila (flore simplici)*, Petit Rosier du Bengale (à fleurs simples)

49 *Rosa Malmundariensis*, Rosier de Malmédy

50 left *Rosa Indica*, La Bengale bichonne; right *Rosa Banksiae*, Rosier de Lady Banks

51 above *Rosa Indica*, Rosier du Bengale (Cent feuilles); below *Rosa Damascena Aurora*, Rosier Aurore Poniatowska

52 left *Rosa Rapa*, Rosier Turneps; right *Rosa Pimpinellifolia rubra (Flore multiplici)*, Rosier Pimprenelle rouge (Variété à fleurs doubles)

53 left *Rosa Gallica Regalis*, Rosier Grandeur Royale; right *Rosa Leucantha*, Rosier à fleurs blanches

54 above *Rosa Alpina flore variegato*, Rosier des Alpes à fleurs panachées; below *Rosa aciphylla*, Rosier cuspidé

55 above *Rosa Pomponia flore subsimplici*, Rosier Pompon à fleurs presque simples; below *Rosa Tomentosa*, Rosier Cotonneux

59 *Rosa Bifera alba*, Rosier des quatre Saisons à fleurs blanches

60 above *Rosa Rubiginosa flore semi-pleno*, Rosier Rouillé à fleurs semidoubles; below *Rosa geminata*, Rosier à fleurs géminées

61 above *Rosa Gallica flore marmoreo*, Rosier de Provins à fleurs marbrées; below *Rosa Dumetorum*, Rosier des Buissons

63 above left *Rosa Pimpinellifolia flore variegato*, La Pimprenelle aux Cent-Ecus; above right *Rosa Gallica agatha (var. Delphiniana)*, L'Enfant de France; below left *Rosa rubiginosa aculeatissima*, Rosier rouillé très épineux; below right *Rosa Pimpinellifolia alba flore multiplici*, Rosier Pimprenelle blanc à fleurs doubles

64 left *Rosa Centifolia crenata*, Rosier Cent feuilles à folioles crenelées; right *Rosa Pumila*, Rosier d'Amour

65 left *Rosa Villosa Terebenthina*, Rosier Velu à odeur de Térébenthine; right *Rosa Multiflora carnea*, Rosier Multiflore à fleurs carnées

66 above *Rosa Inermis*, Rosier Turbiné sans épines; left *Rosa Gallica caerulea*, Rosier de Provins à feuilles bleuâtres; below right *Rosa Campanulata alba*, Rosier Campanulé à fleurs blanches

67 *Rosa mollissima*, Rosier à feuilles molles

68 above *Rosa Longifolia*, Rosier à feuilles de Pêcher; below *Rosa Alpina vulgaris*, Rosier des Alpes commun

69 above *Rosa Spinulifolia Dematratiana*, Rosier Spinulé de Dematra; below *Rosa Myriacantha*, Rosier à Mille-Epines

70 left *Rosa Canina nitens*, Rosier Canin à feuilles luisantes; right *Rosa Multiflora platyphylla*, Rosier Multiflore à grandes feuilles

71 left *Rosa Candolleana Elegans*, Rosier de Candolle; right *Rosa Centifolia Bipinnata*, Rosier à feuilles de Céleri

72 above *Rosa Rubiginosa anemone-flora*, Rosier Rouillé à fleurs d'anémone; below *Rosa Eglanteria Luteola*, L'Eglantier Serin

73 above *Rosa Stylosa*, Rosier des Champs à tiges érigées; below *Rosa Alpina debilis*, Rosier des Alpes à tiges faibles

74 left *Rosa Sempervirens latifolia*, Rosier grimpant à grandes feuilles; right *Rosa centifolia Anglica rubra*, Rosier de Cumberland

75 below *Rosa parvi-flora*, Rosier à petites fleurs; above *Rosa Noisettiana*, Rosier de Philippe Noisette

76 left *Rosa centifolia foliacea*, Rosier à cent feuilles, foliacé; right *Rosa Nivea*, Rosier blanc de Neige

77 left *Rosa Tomentosa*, Rosier Cotonneux; right *Rosa Gallica Granatus*, Rosier de France à Pomme de Grenade

83 *Rosa Hudsoniana Salicifolia* Rosier d'Hudson à feuilles de Saule

84 *Rosa Gallica Agatha incarnata*, L'Agathe Carnée

85 above *Rosa Rubiginosa Vaillantiana*, L'Eglantine de Vaillant; below left *Rosa Eglanteria sub rubra*, L'Eglantier Cerise; right *Rosa Rubifolia*, Rosier à feuilles de Ronce

86 above *Rosa Biserrata*, Rosier des Montagnes à folioles bidentées; below *Rosa Gallica agatha (Varietas parva violacea)*, La petite Renoncule violette

87 above *Rosa Centifolia Burgundiaca*, La Cent-feuilles de Bordeaux; below *Rosa Indica Stelligera*, Le Bengale Etoilé

89 above left *Rosa Indica Sertulata*, Le Bengale à Bouquets; above right *Rosa Pimpinellifolia inermis*, Rosier Pimprenelle a tiges sans épines; below left *Rosa sepium flore submultiplici*, Rosier des hayes à fleurs semi doubles; below right *Rosa Gallica-Agatha (var. Regalis)*, Rosier Agathe-Royale

90 left *Rosa Bifera pumila*, Le petit Quatre-Saisons; above right *Rosa arvensis ovata*, Rosier des champs à fruits ovoïdes; below *Rosa Gallica Stapeliae flora*, Rosier de Provins à fleurs de Stapelie

91 *Rosa Gallica Agatha (var. Prolifera)*, Rosier Agathe Prolifère

92 above *Rosa Indica dichotoma*, La Bengale; below *Rosa Collina Monsoniana*, Rosier de Lady Monson.

93 above *Rosa farinosa*, Rosier farineux; below *Rosa Indica Caryophyllea*, La Bengale Oeillet

94 above *Rosa Gallica Pontiana*, Rosier du Pont; below *Rosa muscosa*, Rosier mousseux

95 left *Rosa Damascena Celsiana prolifera*, Rosier de Cels à fleurs prolifères; right *Rosa Bifera macrocarpa*, La Quatre Saison Lelieur

96 above *Rosa Ventenatiana*, Rosier Ventenat; below *Rosa Reclinata flore simplici*, Rosier à boutons renversés; var. à fleurs simples

97 above *Rosa Gallica Maheka (flore subsimplici)*, Le Maheka à fleurs simples; below *Rosa hispida Argentea*, Rosier hispide à fleurs Argentées

98 left *Rosa Reclinata flore sub multiplici*, Rosier à boutons penchés (var. à fleurs semi doubles); right *Rosa Sepium Myrtifolia*, Rosier des Hayes à feuilles de Myrte

99 left *Rosa l'heritieranea*, Rosier l'héritier; right *Rosa Alba Cimboefolia*, Rosier blanc à feuilles de Chanvre

103 *Rosa Centifolia prolifera foliacea*, La Centfeuilles prolifère foliacée

104 left *Rosa Hudsoniana Subcorymbosa*, Rosier d'Hudson à fleurs presqu'en Corymbe; right *Rosa Rosenbergiana*, Rosier de Rosenberg

105 above *Rosa Centifolia Anemonoïdes*, La Centfeuilles Anémone; below *Rosa Hudsoniana scandens*, Rosier d'Hudson à tiges grimpantes

106 left *Rosa alba foliacea*, La Blanche foliacée de fleury; right *Rosa Gallica Aurelianensis*, La Duchesse d'Orleans

107 left *Rosa Evratina*, Rosier d'Evrat; right *Rosa Gallica (Purpuro-violacea magna)*, Rosier Evêque

108 above *Rosa sempervirens Leschenaultiana*, Le Rosier Leschenault; below *Rosa Gallica Gueriniana*, Rosier Guerin

109 above *Rosa Canina grandiflora*, Rosier Canin à grandes fleurs; below *Rosa Indica Automnalis*, Le Bengale d'Automne

110 below *Rosa Noisettiana purpurea*, Rosier Noisette à fleurs rouges; above *Rosa Bifera Variegata*, La Quatre Saisons à feuilles panachées

111 left *Rosa Indica subalba*, Rosier du Bengale à fleurs blanches; right *Rosa Gallica flore giganteo*, Rosier de Provins à fleur gigantesque

112 left *Rosa Indica fragrans flore simplici*, Le Bengale thé à fleurs simples; right *Rosa Pomponia Burgundiaca*, Le Pompon de Bourgogne

113 left *Rosa Pomponiana muscosa*, Le Pompon mousseaux; right *Rosa Canina Burboniana*, Rosier de l'Ile de Bourbon

All the illustrations are taken from *Les Roses* by Pierre-Joseph Redouté, 1817–24, except for the following (the numbers denote the page numbers):

2, H. Roger-Viollet, Paris
16 above, H. Roger-Viollet, Paris
16 below and 17 below, Bibliothèque Nationale, Paris. Département Cartes et plans
17 above, Bibliothèque Nationale, Paris. Cabinet des estampes
28–29, from *Bon Genre*, Harenberg Kommunikation, Dortmund
40–41, Musée de l'Armée, Paris, Bibliothèque. Photo Free-Lance Photographs, Paris
56–57, Musée Carnavalet. Photo Free-Lance Photographs, Paris
78, Bibliothèque Nationale, Paris. Cabinet des estampes. Photographie Lauros-Giraudon, Paris
79, Musée National de Malmaison. Photographie Lauros-Giraudon, Paris
80 above, Musée National de Malmaison. Photo Laverton, Rueil
80 below, Musée National d'Histoire Naturelle, Paris. Bibliothèque Centrale
80–81, Musée National de Malmaison. Photo Laverton, Rueil
100, Bibliothèque Nationale, Paris
101, Private collection

Στέψον ἐν με καὶ λυρίζω.
Παρὰ σοῖς Διόνυσε, σηκοῖς,
Μετὰ Κύρης βαθυκόλπω,
Ροδίνοισι ςεφανίσκοις,
Πεπυκασμένος χορεύσω.
                    Anacreon Ode V.

Crown me ; of wine the pleasures
Upon my lyre I'll sound,
And with fair maidens measures
Dance, merry and rose-crowned.

Anacreon